MW01296878

TOMORROW, MY SON

September 15, 2021

For my friend Ruth - ask for and you shall receive!

With Love,

A novel based on actual events
by Arlene Lighthall

Edited by Sam French

To my friends, Hermann, Hildegard, and Manfred. They survived. This is their story.

DECEMBER 1995
DEL MAR, CALIFORNIA

Fog hangs low over the breaking waves and curls upon itself as it steadily floats inland along the valley floor. While the surf crashes, it plays with seaweed, tossing it to the left, to the right, forcing it ahead, and eventually dumping it on the shore, just as fate plays with our lives. The salty air is heavy with the odor of fish, as it must have been when my mother sat here 30 years ago. She had come to visit a family who sent care packages to us at the end of World War II, when we were destitute. I wanted to meet those friends myself. I felt close to their son, having corresponded with him for many years and even having worn his outgrown clothes. A copy of my mother's journal, which reveals how a professor and his family became homeless refugees, waits in my backpack as a thank-you gift. Her memories fill more than 20 of those graph paper notebooks so common in Europe. Even though she wrote of long past events, every page reads as if it all happened yesterday.

JULY 1945
SILESIA, GERMANY

I can date my bad dreams back to the days after World War II started but before I had been personally affected by all that was happening in the world and especially in eastern Germany. My husband was beginning to show his concern for my safety, which I had taken for granted.

"Hannah, I have not wanted to talk to you about your trips to the market. I've tried to protect you by not saying anything, but you have probably noticed that the town is changing. More police are posted here than previously. Quite frankly, I'm very nervous each day when I know you are away from the house."

"But Paul. I have to buy our food."

"Maybe I could do the shopping."

"That's ridiculous. Often I don't know what we're going to eat until I get to the market square. Besides, I hardly notice my surroundings when I'm out to get food."

"Ach, Hannah. You are so innocent. I detest the atmosphere created by additional police. I cringe when I see those black, red, and white flags fluttering from public buildings ever since the National Socialists took control of our town. Every year I feel more oppression, right here in Liegenbruch. We hear daily predictions of victory, but what can we expect? The government controls the radio. Yet some people are quietly whispering 'Germany can't win.' It's dangerous for you to be away from home."

"Fritzi's seven now, he's in school, so I'm not needed in the house. You're busy at the university, and I get bored staying at home so much."

"But you are safe here."

"Listening to music and reading are very pleasant pastimes, Paul, but I have to get outside. The only other time I go out alone is to hang clothing on the line."

"Dear wife, those winds that blow the clothes dry may be the last traces of freedom blowing through this town. Please, please! When you are out, do not talk about government and do not ask questions, please!"

"I don't. The only questions I ask are about the freshness of eggs, the price of a piece of veal, or of day-old bread. Usually I see the same housewives shopping, and we don't talk much. The same police officer is always there, too. I mind my own business."

"So much danger lies in just being heard saying anything against the Nazis or about losing the war. I mean not only severe reprisals but even shooting for treason. Do you understand how serious the situation is?"

"I know, I know. Hitler has stirred the hornet's nest, and nearly the whole world is involved. But I don't go to the market square to talk about him or the war."

"I hope the war will not go on much longer, but we really know better. Yes, our country suffered reversals at Stalingrad and El Alemain, but the war theater is immense, nearly beyond my imagination or comprehension. I am so glad that I put aside money to invest in a radio which gets the Allied broadcasts. We can better trust what the British feed us than Goebbel's fodder. Unfortunately our reliable atlas is not highly detailed, so I have to guess the sites of some battles and advances."

"Yes, Professor Merkel. I get the point."

At times I felt a twinge of guilt while listening to English newscasts. I didn't understand everything I heard, yet was amazed we had such freedom. The Nazis must not have felt threatened or surely they would have confiscated our only path to the world outside the Reich. Daily life continued unchanged, relatively untouched by the surrounding turmoil. Surprisingly we were able to think of the conflicts as being "there" and we were "here."

The clock dictated our days. Breakfast was promptly at 0800, and usually an easy meal: toast, cherry or plum jam, a hard-cooked egg, coffee, and milk. I always used Paul's pretty blue and white cups and plates. At 08:42 I would see Paul and Fritzi off for the morning. Tidying up and cleaning and laundry occurred between 08:45 and 09:45. I was never at the market any later than 10:00 to buy provisions for our rich, mid-day meal. Paul's favorites were beef rolls, potatoes, peas, and cherries with cream, or on other occasions red cabbage, potatoes, gravy and sauerbraten. I always served the evening meal at 17:30. Standardizing our days this way helped preserve our sense of security, normality, and regularity, which had begun to erode.

From spring through fall I planted and weeded vegetables, watched seeds sprout, pruned shrubs and trees, transplanted, picked, and canned fruits and vegetables. My mother had prepared me well for this domestic life. Nothing broke the routine. Although we were a married couple, each of us had our work to keep us occupied. Oh, I was aware of the winds of change, but also I was powerless to change them.

The military often strutted through the market square like elites in their gray uniforms, wide black belts, and pants tucked into high boots. While I didn't understand their ranks or insignia, I did know that I didn't want to get too close to them. I wondered why so many more police were stationed in town. To keep order among us housewives? I could sense unease among the women shopping.

One day I was disturbed when the policeman usually stationed in the square began to follow me. I had done nothing to arouse his suspicions, but he certainly made me uncomfortable. Knowing the SS had absorbed the national police, we couldn't trust their protection. Anyway, those officers came from other sectors of the Reich. Like all Germans in some type of military service they loved their uniforms. So I heeded Paul's warning: "The slightest hint of indiscretion could get you shot."

"*Guten tag,*" he addressed me. I nodded, going about my shopping. A swastika pin gleamed on his lapel. When he wasn't following me, he sat on some crates watching us shoppers. Every day I had to pass by a small pub near the square and frequently saw him entering or leaving.

His little greetings continued for several weeks until one day he approached me.

"May I invite you to join me for a Pils?"

"No, danke. I don't drink alcohol."

"Then a coffee, perhaps?"

"No, danke."

"You may not know it, but beer is a very nutritious food. I always have one to start my day and then two more in the morning to keep up my strength and to keep me alert."

Throwing his cigarette on the ground, he lit another before trying to take my bag from me.

"Here, let me carry that for you. A pretty woman like you shouldn't be loaded like a mule."

"No, danke. You must certainly have more important duties."

"Nein, nein," he insisted. "I'll carry it home for you."

I didn't know what to do. The police had unlimited power. That man could fabricate all kinds of lies about me, and I would have no defense. His attentions were alarming.

He forcefully took my net bag from my hand, and at first I feared he was going to steal it. I noticed his nicotine stained yellow fingers were still grasping a cigarette. After he had smoked it down to the very butt, he asked me to hold my bag while he lit up again, offering me a "smoke."

"Nein."

"You may wonder why I want with you to talk. It is because you remind me of my wife and because you look like a very intelligent woman. My Liz is a very good person and an excellent cook and housekeeper. She were always busy cleaning. I guess she feels inferior when I am with others talking. Moreover, she cannot make friends as quickly as I can. Perhaps because she is my second wife she thinks I am shopping for a third, just as you shop for groceries. It is not my fault that women are attracted to me. I can tell you are like her. You feel inferior and like me for a friend."

My silence didn't dissuade him. I made no reply and kept walking.

"You see, we just met and already we are good friends. You mustn't feel inferior. I always can make friends easily."

Up until this day my life had always been predictable. Now that previous security was endangered. We Germans had always been raised to respect authority. Even though the Nazis had caused us to revise those ingrained concepts at a national level, here I was meeting a challenge in my own neighborhood. I had never paid much attention to men. Except for Paul, they all seemed rather neuter, and aroused no particular emotions. But this unintelligent, uninformed man was repulsive. He turned comfort to chaos. I detested all he had to say and stood for. And a married man! He accompanied me home ANYWAY.

AUGUST 1944

I couldn't understand why the policeman had targeted me for his attentions, or perhaps he pestered other women as well.

"Do you like to dance? Every German woman likes to dance, no matter how young or old. Do you have a husband? If your husband doesn't like to, maybe I could take you to the dance hall some night."

I had never told him anything. It was none of his business. I hadn't even told him my name, that I was married, or about my child. I wanted nothing to do with that man and was not going to encourage him with conversation.

On another day he again took my bag. I was becoming extremely irritated by his incessant chatter and embarrassed to be seen with him. He was a loutish braggart. He was smothering and overbearing. Had he used a megaphone, his voice wouldn't have carried any further. I felt helpless with no place to complain. After all, he was a policeman.

"Do you like to travel?"

No reply.

"I like to see new places. I'll pay a visit to my friends in California, the more so since the expenses do not matter at all. What I am interested in is to converse with sophisticated people like you, but as much to go for sight-seeing and to go to objects of interest like the Redwoods, Indian reservations, thus objects which have grown by nature or history. I don't have time to tell you how I made friends with people from California. Not this time."

Would this never end? Again he walked with me to the front of the house. I thanked him, took my bags, and went inside. After several weeks of putting up with him, I felt overwhelmed by his attentions, suffocated, but I was afraid of upsetting Paul by telling him.

That day I was putting a plate of boiled potatoes on the table for our noonday meal, along with some chicken and boiled cabbage when Paul came home. He was becoming morose. He couldn't discuss political topics with most of his colleagues, and those who shared his sentiments sent him home with paralyzed will, shattered nerves. When I tried to present a more positive view, I met little success. He asked how educated people could see the situation any differently.

"Hitler has solidified his power. At first his criminal clique amused us with its frivolity. We could not take those jokesters seriously."

He had assumed his professorial tone. I was going to remind him that the architect Speer was an educated man, but I dared not lest he start on his father's plans for him again. Perhaps some hot food would cheer him and take his mind off the subject. I was tempted to tell him about the walk home, but that was not the time.

Once, when the policeman invited conversation, I looked at his flushed, pockmarked face and saw a scar on his left cheek. His complexion was ruddy; his hair was reddish-blond. Although he was a large man, he was not as tall as Paul and much more stocky, barrel-chested, his stomach bloated by beer. Even fat. His cigarette breath was fetid, as bad as summer garbage infested with maggots.

"You may wonder how I came by this scar on my cheek," he commented, throwing a cigarette butt into the street.

No, I wasn't interested. I hated to hear his loud boasts.

"It's a battle scar. In Cologne I ran into two ragamuffins to rob a store one night. Both were much larger than I am, but I'm powerful and know how to fight. I knocked one to the ground and was wrestling with him when he pulled a knife on me. I got this scar, but I captured him and we later arrested his friend. He had to run away, probably scared by my hand-to-hand fighting and my strength. I received a special commendation for this courage."

Not responding, I went into the house.

SEPTEMBER 1944

I dared not tell Paul about the policeman lest he forbid my going out. He had become more distrustful of the political situation each day, and when he didn't share his thoughts with me, he brooded. I recall I hadn't been pregnant very long, nearly eight years ago, when one day he said he wanted to talk seriously.

"Hannah, I am torn with such turmoil. One part of me warns that we should leave Germany, get out before that criminal ruins our country and our lives. His rising power frightens me. The other part says that this is the only life we know. We might be able to make a difference somewhere down the line if we stay."

I told him he was much more aware than I of the political situation in Germany and I would rely on his assessment.

"What do you hear your colleagues saying?"

"I hate to tell you. They say Hitler will save us, that Germany will rise again. One would expect more enlightenment from so-called educated people. Of course, I hold my tongue."

"But, Paul, if we left, where would we go? When?"

"I do not know. I wish I knew. I have asked myself those same questions so many times." He ran his fingers through his thick hair over and over. Then he lowered his head, grasping it on both sides as if in grief.

"I am afraid it might be dangerous to leave. You are in a delicate condition. I cannot risk losing the dream of my life, to have a child, maybe even a son. What madness to bring a child into our chaotic world!"

Back and forth he went. From one solution to another problem, like a scientist testing various hypotheses, not knowing which one to pursue first. He was the man. It was his decision, and I trusted him. He lacked faith in our government and feared repression.

Three days later I had another experience with the policeman.

"You may wonder why I mention how I make friends so easily. Let me tell you how I made friends in southern Germany. My wife and her cousin were on holiday in Italy so the cousin's husband, Wolfgang, and I decided to go south to places which I know so well that I even did not need a map for a three-day holiday. In Rothenberg *ob der Tauber* we could make friends with two pretty and sophisticated Japanese girls, both well-behaved and obviously fairly rich. They even tried to refuse that I paid their meals, but at least I could persuade them by telling that I would cheat a rich farmer the difference for my expenses to pay."

My curiosity was piqued. He must have taken my look at him as an invitation to continue.

"Oh, I used to could make drawings for constructions. I made a lot of money. I'm not a *nassauer* either."

I said nothing.

"Do you know what a *nassauer* is? No, I can tell you don't know. A *nassauer* is a person who is never ready to pay when he is together with some friends in a pub or restaurant. As soon as it were time to pay, he has always vanished to the toilet or elsewhere. He says he must tend the horses. His friends must then pay while he is gone. Or he is a person who never has his own cigarettes."

He had taken my shopping bag and then asked me to hold it while he lit a cigarette and offered me one.

"My wife is still suffering from an injury she had last year. She cycled on the main street over a crossing. She had the right of law. But she was pushed violently by a car from a side. The driver had not given way. She got flung through the air and came down on the bonnet of the car. After the car stopped, she had fell slowly to the ground. Her left collarbone and four ribs were broken but are gradually healing. Luckily she is much better now but cannot yet make any works with her left arm. This injury also made her feel inferior because she cannot keep the house as usual clean, so she is downcast. Since you are a woman, I am sure that you understand how she can feel when she cannot so busy with housework be. We have no children to tire her, so she were complaining that I cannot stay at home with her and now that am stationed here away from her.

"After all, in spite of the injury, she were very lucky. The young girl driver said, 'I can pay the bike.' Her mother was in the car and said Liz were foolish to be riding a bicycle on a busy street. She added, 'It were an old bike.'

"Those fools. The sick fund will charge an amount of 3,000 ostmarks at least from the girl's insurance, and our solicitor will charge about the same amount, plus his fee! And those fools might have thought the case were finished after they brought some flowers and declared to be ready to pay some 20 ostmarks for an old bike. They even didn't their insurance inform until they got a letter from our solicitor. They didn't know I was a policeman and very shrewd. I didn't mind that it might cost me more than the return. I could afford the sum. I can tell you are an intelligent woman. You don't ride a bicycle to the market and try on it to take a heavy bag."

By the time he had finished this long monologue, we had arrived at my house. I was glad to escape inside, wishing I could take Paul's suggestion that he shop and I stay at home. How I wished I could talk to him!

Evenings after Fritzi went to bed, Paul and I usually read in the living room. Although I was often tired from a busy work day, I delayed going to bed too early because the events of my days were beginning to invade my nights. The bad dreams usually disappeared quickly, and I had trouble recalling the details. What I did remember was an overwhelming feeling of impotence, of situations out of my control, of being an alien in an unfamiliar world.

OCTOBER 1944

My bad dreams continued in the same vein and were causing an hour or more of lost sleep each night. I tried not to disturb Paul by leaving the bed, and I doubt he was aware of my state.

During the following days, I tried to hurry from vendor to vendor in an attempt to escape the policeman. No luck.

"I don't believe I've told you my name. You may call me Hermann."

I didn't answer.

He pulled off a glove, saying, "Look at this hand."

I saw a long scar on his wrist, almost as if someone started to cut off his hand. Another slash ran towards his fingers. Then he pulled back his shirt sleeve.

"You may wonder how I came by this scar on my arm. It's from another fight with a criminal. I went to a doctor, and he told me that I were not go home immediately after the surgery, that it could be perilous for the wound. Of course, I knew that with a gypsum bandage I could not drive myself. So I had asked ahead of time a neighbor's wife to take me there and to drive me home. Women have always been quite happy to do things for me. Usually I don't even have to ask."

He paused, looking steadily at me.

"After the doctor were finished, the medical assistant told me that I were going to have terrible pain in the hand, though only for a brief time. Well, on our way home--the local anesthesia were not yet over--we paid a short visit at English friends of mine who used to live in Erkelenz. They thought I should have a good medicine against the pain that I had to expect. They gave me a big beer-glass full of whiskey, and after I finished it, a second one. Strange enough to say, I were not tipsy at all, but also did not feel any pain in the hand, neither the same nor the following days."

I had bought provisions for several days on that occasion to avoid a few days' harassment and hoping he would find another object for his attentions. No luck! He again latched onto me, walking very briskly so that I had trouble keeping up, but I had to because he had my bag. Once I had tried walking very fast, trying to get home quickly, the sooner to brush away the pest buzzing in my ear.

"You may wonder how a big man like me can walk so fast," he began again at top volume for everyone within earshot to hear.

"I myself for many years have gone for a walk every day, in rubber boots, of course. I always used to walk very fast and up to 15K a day. It were very healthy for me. Just like it is very healthy to drink beers. Even in the coldest weather I didn't need gloves nor did I keep my hands in my pockets, even at a temperature of 10 degrees centigrade. I guess that were mainly because I walked so fast and moved my arms . . . some 7K an hour over bumpy frozen snow . . . .

"But after a few weeks that 'training' were over. One day when I went home, I felt a pain in my right foot. It were swollen so that I could hardly get out of my boot. One or two days later, I could feel with my fingers that one of the bones in the middle of my foot were broken, and I don't even know when and where it could happen. I did not go to the doctor's for this bagatelle, since I thought it came by itself and would also heal by itself, and moreover, there are four other bones more that would keep my foot the right way. So I continued my walks, though only the necessary ones, while stepping down only on my right heel. After some two weeks all trouble were over, so I am sure that my way of 'repairing' a broken foot bone is better than three or four weeks with my foot in gypsum!"

Would he ever shut up? I found him more unbearable each day. Why wouldn't the repulsive creature let me be?

Yet again he shouted, "You may wonder why I walk with you through the streets." I didn't answer.

"I tell the other officers that you are a cousin. They believe me, of course, because I am shrewd in deception. Shall we stop for a croquette or a Pils?"

"No thank you."

I wondered if I should tell Paul about him. But what could he do? He would just worry or demand that I stay at home. Hermann took my arm with his free hand. I was offended and pretended to point to something and talked with my hands and waved my arms a bit and was very nervous and scared. Soon he let go. I began walking even faster; in fact, I nearly ran, keeping somewhat ahead of him.

At top volume so that everyone on the street could hear, he began again, splashing spittle on me.

"I can tell that you are a very intelligent woman and I am a very intelligent man. That must be why we are attracted to each other."

I was flabbergasted and so embarrassed. Then he put a hand on my arm again, and I was gripped with dread and revulsion as I grabbed my bags and said "Danke." He followed me all the way to the door this time and forced his way in. I told him he should leave at once, but he took the bags from me and put them on the floor at the foot of the stairs. He grabbed me and forced me to look at that terrible face asking for "just a little kiss."

I pushed him away, screaming, "Mein Gott! Do you take me for a common street whore? Let me go!"

My protests were loud enough to bring Fritzi from his room upstairs. I thank the Lord I hadn't gotten to the kitchen with the provisions. Otherwise Fritzi couldn't have heard me.

"Mutti, Mutti, what's the matter?"

I had kept him home from school because he had a fever, one of many he would suffer in coming years. Hermann let me go, surprised by the child. I thanked him for his help carrying my packages, and he left. The situation had become so precarious I could no longer protect Paul from what was happening.

After supper when Fritzi was in bed, we discussed the uniformed bully.

"Paul, I'm vulnerable, defenseless. What can I do?"

"There is no denying that the police are omnipotent. I cannot let you shop alone any more. I was right all along."

"But I don't see any of our neighbors at the market when I'm there. Otherwise we could go together."

"We must face the facts. Going to someone in authority to complain will accomplish nothing except to make the policeman want revenge on us."

"Yes, he could denounce me for having made some treasonous remark."

"And you know how dangerous that is. Ach, mein Gott. To think that this is happening in our town! Law, order, justice--empty words today."

"Oh, Paul, I'm so frightened. The market square is only a 15-minute walk from here in one direction and the university is the same distance in the other. I can't be asking you to spend half an hour away from your work to shop while I hide here at home."

"No, I shall go with you. The market opens at seven. We shall go together early instead of your going around ten. Then I shall walk home again with you. Lock the doors as soon as you are back in the house."

"I can prepare Fritzi's breakfast before we leave. I won't be so fussy about the quality of the vegetables so I'll take less time at the market stands."

"We can arrive home before Fritzi leaves for school. I shall walk with him as usual."

"I can try to buy a few more items at a time so we'd have to go only three times a week instead of every day."

"Good plan. And, Hannah, you do not have to be such a meticulous housekeeper. Some days you can go with me. You would like that, would you not?"

"Oh, how I would! Back to the library, or maybe even helping you in the lab. But what about our meals?"

"Keep in mind that my school is in the opposite direction from the market. You could return home in time to prepare our noon meal. I doubt that the policeman could get himself stationed in front of our house."

"You know I can't trust any neighbors with this dilemma. Gossip on the street has probably already started. I hate that man. He's probably tarnished my reputation."

"Well, my dear, I think we may have solved our problem for the time being. It is getting late. Time to sleep."

We followed our new routine for several weeks. It took adjusting on the part of all three of us, but the effort was worthwhile. My nightmares were fewer, and I didn't jump in alarm at the slightest unusual noise. All of us neighbors kept to ourselves. I wasn't accustomed to knocks at the door.

Meanwhile, the situation at the frontlines was demanding more and more troops to hold off the invading Russians. Paul heard that some police had been transferred. One day we changed our routine by going to the market later in the morning. Hermann was   gone.

NOVEMBER 1944

I often thought about how I got here from the farm where I grew up. As a young girl, I was too naive and inexperienced to have opinions about anything. Like a blade of grass blowing in a breeze, I swayed to and fro with no plan for the direction my life should take.

At the local school I received high marks in all of my classes. Science, literature, and art were my favorites. An unmarried science teacher there, *Fraulein* Keppler, encouraged me to continue my studies. No one in my family had an advanced education. How ridiculous for a girl! A luxury! Unheard of in my small village! A waste of family resources! A joke! Schooling was for sons. A daughter should remain close to her parents and marry a good Lutheran man. My folks relentlessly grieved for years the loss of my brother in World War I. They didn't want to lose me.

Fraulein Keppler's confidence was flattering, and she had a long talk with my parents. Their hold on me was very strong, my being the only child left. Fortunately, their love was also very strong, and they relented, releasing me from my sense of guilt.

After finishing at the gymnasium, I enrolled in the small University of Liegenbruck, where *Fraulein* Keppler continued financing my education. I was a tall, skinny beanpole with straight blond hair, plain as water, ignored by the boys. My skin was clear and pale, my cheeks were peach-colored rather than rosy, and my eyes were as clear blue as a mountain lake.

My clothing? Well, it was simple, cheap, unfashionable, serviceable, consisting of a few woolen skirts, a green sweater plus two plain-colored blouses that went with the skirts, one print dress, and a *louden* heavy coat. It was what my parents could afford. In short, no one would stop for a second look at me.

Near the campus I rented a room from an elderly couple, Herr and Frau Klemper, who supplemented his pension by taking in students. Their children were grown and had families of their own in other cities. Herr Klemper was in poor health, often in bed, so I really didn't see much of him.

I paid my monthly rent, and we greeted each other as I came and went, but there was little socializing. I was busy with classes and studying during the day and ate a warm midday meal on the campus. After the Klempers had eaten supper, I returned to my room, where some simple food on a tray waited for me: bread and cold cuts and cheese and a pickle. My life was routine and satisfactory. I was determined to succeed as a scholar because I couldn't let down my parents or my former teacher.

After Paul and I married, we moved into this flat where he had lived for years. It was a long and narrow unit at the end of a brick apartment building, so we had side windows in addition to the ones from the living room to the street. I liked the two kitchen windows from which I could admire our fruit trees and watch my vegetable garden prosper.

Paul had lived alone and furnished the flat to his taste. He hadn't collected clutter through those many years. Each week I cleaned the two bedrooms and bath upstairs one day and downstairs the next. In between I dusted and tidied up.

From our front door led a long hallway to the kitchen, larger than most but containing the common electric appliances, a table, and four chairs. Paul's pride was an antique white porcelain stove, at least 60 years old but in pristine condition. It reached nearly to the ceiling and burned both coal and wood from an opening at the bottom. Over the kitchen sink and again over the bathtub upstairs water tanks heated five liters at a time. A small half-bathroom was off the kitchen.

Above the kitchen was a loft used for drying clothes and storage of old clothing and rags. The living and dining rooms flanked the front entrance hallway, each closed from the hall by a door and heated separately. It was practical and economical for us to heat a room only if we were using it and to keep the doors to the hall closed. In the living room we had our bookcases, a record player, Paul's desk, an easy chair for reading, and a comfortable sofa. The traditional pot of flowers sat on the window ledge just outside lace curtains. Their dense pattern of roses with extra long leaves prevented passersby from looking into the house. Next to the front door, to the right, stairs went up.

This was a comfortable home. I enjoyed caring for it. Paul's prohibiting my leaving the house would have trapped me like a bug in a jar.

And then a worse thought: was I trapped in a marriage? I had never known another man, never had what is called a boyfriend. Paul was a fine man. Had he ever loved another woman? What is love, anyway? He was now over 50. Had I been the only woman available? Had he been looking for a healthy Aryan woman to mother his child? Was he the only man available for me? Ach, this was not the time for uncertainty, to teeter on the taut rope leading from an innocent past to today's precarious security. I thought back on the time I first saw him.

1930 TO 1935

While I was at the university, Professor Paul Merkel was my chemistry professor--a tall bachelor in his mid 40's. His features were regular--somewhat square chin, slightly pointed nose. He was very handsome in his way, with thick blond hair and grey-blue eyes like frosty ice on a pond in winter. His eyes told us students as much as his words. When one of us gave an incorrect answer, he would open his eyes quite wide. No words were needed. He lifted his eyebrows and lowered his forehead in consternation if someone waited too long to respond.

What I liked best was his smile. We could see his pleasure when the corners of his mouth turned up slightly. I don't think he ever laughed in class or even smiled showing all of his teeth. On the other hand, he never lost his temper with us or embarrassed anyone. His was a gentle nature, and all of us were very fond of him in spite of the strict discipline he demanded.

His lectures were always well organized, and when he entered the hall, we students became silent at his towering presence: long, determined steps to the lectern, a folder of notes in his hand, though he seldom referred to them after he began to lecture slowly and distinctly.

He started the class when the clock stopped striking the hour. No one would think of coming in late. Almost always he wore a dark gray suit with either a white or gray shirt. The variety in his dress came with changing neckties. Occasionally he appeared in his white lab coat.

I followed the prescribed curriculum for four years and graduated with honors. To attend the ceremony, my parents came to the university for the first time. Although the farm was not far away, they were busy. My mother's eyes flooded with tears of pride as I stood holding my diploma.

"My dear daughter. I am so proud of you. Just think! A daughter with a university degree."

"What comes next in your life?" asked my father with a quivering lower lip. I think both of them were uneasy. There was no work for me near our small village unless I were to wait until some teacher in the gymnasium retired or died. At any rate, my steps would not lead back there. But what would I do? I never had dreams or fantasies about my future. It always seemed to take care of itself.

I explained to them, "My science professor needs help in his lab and has invited me to assist him. Nothing is certain yet because I have to be approved by his superior."

"And is he married?" my mother wanted to know, "and how old is he?"

Laughing I told them that he was a bachelor and quite elderly, about 50 years old.

"Haven't you found any promising young man to court you here?" queried my father, possibly worrying that I would return to being a dependent.

I looked down, embarrassed, feeling great affection for both of my parents and also a sense I had disappointed them in not making a good match in these years away.

"I wasn't here to look for a husband but to get a good education and to learn how to earn my own living. I've accomplished my goal to learn, and we shall have to see about my occupation or profession."

Growing up, I was never invited to parties; at the university I really had no social life or special friends except for books and Professor Merkel. Some women wore their hair in permanent waves from a beauty parlor. I had a straight bob; it was easier to care for. Never did I find in my purse spare money for stylish clothing. In fact, I never wore a "proper" hat until years later when I was married. A knitted cloche was good enough, or a woolen head scarf that I could tuck under my coat collar to make a sort of hood to ward off cold winds.

I was flattered by my professor's invitation to work in his lab but was a bit nervous about the interview. The department chief was a very pleasant man and seemed to like me, but he warned, "Professor Merkel is a very attractive man, and he could have many women, but he isn't interested in getting married."

I was amused and responded, "I also am not interested in finding a husband."

Lab work was very routine and exacting. By nature, perhaps like most Germans, I was good at organization and prided myself on how I kept my papers and books and equipment. I liked the sense of order my work demanded. The professor was a patient man, so gentle in explaining my tasks. So business-like.

Little by little, we became better acquainted with each other, but ours was strictly a professional relationship. He was Herr Professor or Professor Merkel. I was *Fraulein* Vogelsang. He was friendly but aloof. Science was his focus as it was mine. I had known little of the lives of my classmates, let alone that of my professor. He hired me as his assistant and not his confidant.

One day I was quite surprised when I heard him mutter, "My father wanted me to have a career in commerce."

I realized a human being was in the white lab coat, not a robotic technician.

"I did not aspire to a commercial career," he continued complaining in his usual formal diction. "He was a prominent architect in Hasselhof. He wanted to push me around as he did the walls and windows in his renderings. I had no desire to spend a lifetime designing factories as he did nor in the business world. My passion was science."

"Couldn't your mother help you to persuade him?" I asked timidly.

"She was a musician, a pianist from the south, and died before the melodies from her life filtered down into mine. In my own way, I am as Prussian as my father. He works with simple lines, order, function. Here in the lab, details, precise records, method--all the same kind of Germanic order. But I shall not leave behind any monuments."

"What kind of monuments do you mean?"

"They probably would not mean anything to you, but he designed the Hassel knife factory, the Roempagel garment works, the Schmidt canning factory, and other commercial buildings. I said 'monuments,' but my father's is a temporary legacy. Tastes change and bricks crumble."

Perhaps fearing he revealed too much, at this point he left the lab.

My time was not completely devoted to science. Living close to the university, I was able to enjoy many cultural events as well as performances by the city's orchestra. The theater was special and usually presented the wonderful old classics by Lessing and Hauptmann.

Even though I continued living with the Klempers, the university's library became my true home. There I escaped from the bare room I rented to anywhere in the world I wanted to go. Art books took me to galleries in Italy. I was an adventurer in remote lands. The Far East was so foreign to anything I had ever known that it seemed I often didn't mentally return to Germany for days. Maps were my obsession and catapulted me across continents. With volumes beckoning me, I had no need for friends.

Part of my small salary each month went to my parents and to my former teacher, who had made possible my new life. I even spent some on myself, usually at a bookstore. A new dark brown sweater was affordable and practical. Like a young lad tossing a stone into a brook and laughing to see it splash and disappear, I tossed with equal glee my ragged green sweater into a trash bin.

For four years I stayed on in the lab, lacking the gumption to try anything different. The professor gradually entrusted me with more complex tasks. Tending the lab as he had it organized was easy for me since I was one of those people who believed in "a place for everything and everything in its place." We got along well, from time to time sharing parts of our lives but always intent upon our research. Gradually the outside came in.

"That man is a dangerous fiend, a fanatic," he declared one day. "His hypnotic power over our people frightens me; it is demonic. . . . And those weak-minded little people have helped him seize control."

I always had the impression he was lecturing when he spoke to me. His speech was formal, his vocabulary elevated, and he seldom used contractions. Did he mean one of his superiors at the university? I truly didn't know what he was talking about, or rather preaching and muttering to himself.

"I don't understand. What people? Who's dangerous? What control?"

I felt ashamed when he raised his eyebrows before answering, "Why, I'm talking about Hitler and his rise to power."

On he went, "He preaches the grandiose glory of Germany's distant past. How I cringe as the masses rejoice at rallies! And those people swell with pride when they see swastika flags waving! In their homes they are thrilled to hear his voice on the radio! He promises that the Nazi party will solve all the problems of our people. Ach, I find it all revolting."

His monologue was so unlike the usual conversations we had but more formal as his lectures had been.

"What enlightened person can enjoy Wagner any more? He did not compose his music for the party. Now it is propaganda for pride in the Aryan race."

I'd always enjoyed hearing Wagner's music and never connected it with anything political.

He continued in his professorial tone, "National pride is another poison infecting our people. Many lost their pride when we lost the war in 1918. I fear the inevitability of war and the proportions to which that mad man will be driven. His promises have hypnotized citizens into virtual slavery. A war will not free us."

"A war!" I exclaimed, astounded.

I'll never forget Professor Merkel's look of incredulity as he lifted his brows again. I respected him as my superior and as a person of experience, considering his age. He seemed to look straight through me, as if I were a shadowy film. Where had I been? I felt like an admonished pupil.

My life had been so filled with work and escape into books that I had no awareness of the political situation in Germany. My parents had never been interested in the world outside their farm. At times I believe they regretted permitting me to get an education beyond the gymnasium, to accept aid. Once my mother said I had grown away from them and the family, but my father, perhaps more correctly, said, "I don't think we ever had her."

They were rather impoverished potato farmers, always complaining they should have been growing beets. Politics held little interest for them since all their energy went into the earth, which sapped their strength but at least kept them alive. I had never been prepared for world affairs and never had any interest in the government. During my university years I studied and read only my texts.

Listening to the professor, I realized how ignorant I was, paying no attention to what was happening in my country. I had entombed myself in the library, surrounded by books filled with the past. I listened to the rhythms of poetry, romantically escaping my everyday world. I felt balanced. Science by day and art by night. I didn't need more.

"Ach, Hannah," I reprimanded myself. "You think you're an educated woman. You're a book learner. You memorize and recite back. You're living in a past that never existed, a present that you don't even know, and you're unconsciously drifting into a stormy future."

From that day I began my new education in politics, the problems of poverty, and inflation. I started to read newspapers, to eavesdrop on conversations in the streets, to notice shops had been vacated, and to listen and to learn while working in the lab. From time to time Professor Merkel invited me to have an afternoon coffee. I always enjoyed those outings, when I usually had apple tart with coffee and rich whipped cream. He often had a beer. I could converse with more confidence about our country and what was happening, and he patiently answered my questions with that rather shy smile I liked to see.

A street near the university used to be a one-lane country road. Located only a few steps from the pavement stood a stone and half-timbered pub, built centuries ago. In olden times, houses and businesses abutted the road, a special advantage when snow was deep. I'd always wanted to walk through the front door of that pub with its amber glass panels, but felt it wasn't a place for a young girl alone. Professor Merkel commented as we finished work on a rainy afternoon that he would enjoy a stein of beer and that I might enjoy visiting that pub. Of course, I would.

We entered, crossing a flagstone floor, and felt a warmth emanating from the iron sconces on the walls and pewter lamps on pedestal bases. Horseshoes and copper pots hung on the wall flanking a mounted deer's head. Stained glass windows that weren't visible from the street made me forget the gloom outside.

We walked past a suit of armor, a ball and mace, enormous copper kettles, iron candlesticks filled with burning candles--my eyes couldn't take in everything this museum held for them. Toward the back, our destination was a black square island counter composed of brick-shaped stones. It was too dark to see clearly an old framed map, and I expressed my regrets.

"I'd like a closer look at that map. I may have told you that maps have been an obsession ever since I was a child and learned how places were located on a paper."

The professor smiled. "It's probably been in that frame and hung in that spot for several hundred years. I suppose guests consulted it as they stopped here for a meal or night's lodging."

Edith, the waitress, had overheard our conversation and seemed well acquainted with my teacher. He introduced me as his assistant and told me that she had been working at the pub for 48 years.

"If you like the old map," she offered, "you may also want to look at the guest book before you leave."

What a work of art it was, with its 3/4-inch-thick cover of leather and carved wood. Pictured on the front was a brigand pouring beer from a pitcher into a mug. Inside, names of guests starting with stays in the 16th century sprang forth. I would never forget the excitement of that afternoon.

We returned to the black counter to finish our afternoon snack. The back area was empty except for us--too early for the evening drinkers.

"*Fraulein*, I would be very pleased if you could call me 'Paul.' We have worked together now for four years and could put our friendship on a more intimate level."

Naturally I didn't expect this and was speechless for a few minutes. First names were used only among family members or very close friends. What could this handsome man see in me to ask me to call him "Paul"?

"Yes, Paul, that would be very nice."

"And I hope you won't mind if I call you 'Hannah.'"

"Not at all."

Soon we picked up our umbrellas from the stand at the front door. The rain had stopped. We walked past several stores that had been empty, open again under new ownership. It seemed the town was returning to normal.

"These shops used to be owned by Jews," Paul told me, "but now party members have taken them over. There never were many Jews in the area, and I assume that they left because of their opposition to the wave of national socialism."

I listened carefully to all he told me, and each day I became more aware of what was happening around me. Experiments in the lab and our conversations about the worsening situation in Germany continued for several months.

I was a little nervous calling him "Paul" after so many years of our formal relationship, but it gradually became more comfortable. I liked being with him. I admired him. I listened and learned and eventually loved. But did I know love? Did I feel passion? Lust? Overwhelming desire? How it all happened still perplexes me. One day, when he unexpectedly proposed, I agreed. It was as natural a thing to do as to fill a test tube for a new experiment.

My parents wanted us to marry in my home village to the north, but I'd been away for so long that I knew no one there I wanted to invite. My favorite teacher, Frau Keppler, had passed away. I'm glad that I completely repaid her while she was alive.

The civil ceremony took place in Liegenbruck with a few of Paul's colleagues in attendance. My parents were pleased that I had "made such a fine match," but they were disappointed, too, because I wouldn't be living near them.

Paul was a good provider. Our conversations early in the marriage hadn't started to center on the topic of leaving the country. National events didn't touch us personally, and we seemed to have settled into complacency.

When I left my job, I exchanged my white lab coat for a Kittelschürze, a sleeveless smock that covers from the shoulders to the knees and buttons up the front. This type of uniform makes the German housewife look like domestic help in her own home, a situation that is probably close to the truth. In my case, however, I didn't feel that way.

Later I learned that in the U.S. women wear aprons, which may be very fancy with lace and embroidery or quite plain, just barely covering a dress, either from the shoulders or from the waist. They had aprons for everyday and very fancy ones for entertaining. I think we German women are more honest, all wearing the same kind of uniform instead of trying to disguise our position with frills. I contented myself being a hausfrau and a mother.

1936 TO 1941

Not long after the wedding, my thin body began to swell. My only concern was my threadbare winter coat, which would no longer button easily, though I am not sure that Paul even noticed. But his joy in my condition was almost manic.

"I'll be a father! I've never known such happiness," he exclaimed with tears in his eyes. I didn't know what was greatest: my joy in becoming a mother, his joy in becoming a father, or my joy in so pleasing my husband.

Paul was very protective and worried I might overdo. Both of us were healthy, tall people, he over two meters, and I was only somewhat shorter. It was an easy pregnancy, probably because of my large bone structure. No morning sickness. No falling asleep afternoons or after supper. After nine months Fritzi dropped quickly. He was a large baby, 23 inches long. The birthing was so easy I planned to have many more, but more were unthinkable in those disturbing times.

We watched our son crawl, become a toddler, learn to talk, to walk. His life was my life. He was about two years old when Hitler invaded Poland in September 1939. We had no idea to what extent the fanatic's ambition would drive him. At the market, over the milk pails, I heard whispers of an extended war. Should we leave? Could we leave? Paul had stopped questioning.

Nearly every day Fritzi and I walked to the nearby pond, which was especially lovely, inhabited by swans and ducks. He took a jar one day to catch some pollywogs for pets.

"I have three, Mutti, and I'm going to call them Curly, Lucky, and Cutie."

He was very proud of his new pets and persuaded Paul to go with him to get another three because Curly wanted more company than the two with him. They returned, smiling and chuckling.

"Look here, Mutti, what we have: six more plus three tiny frogs."

The jar was large, but hardly big enough for the growing collection. One frog got away while Fritzi changed the water; another was dead one morning; and yet another was literally eaten alive under our very eyes by a large pollywog. That night Fritzi cried at bedtime, upset because his pets had to sleep downstairs in the kitchen instead of in his room where he could protect them.

It took little time for him to realize that such pets would not last long out of their natural environment, so we returned them to the pond. Fritzi decided to make a picture book of the pollywogs, but in order for it to be authentic, he would have to take paper and pencils to the pond, to draw them where they lived.

On winter weekends we enjoyed family outings to ice skate on the frozen pond or in warmer weather to picnic along the river banks. Fritzi brought great joy into our lives. He was a bashful boy with downcast eyes and his father's slight smile. Perhaps being the only son of older parents made him rather shy and less boisterous than other children. He would be a tall man, like his father. Already he was taller than his schoolmates, though much thinner. It seemed I never could get extra flesh on his bones, no matter how much food I fed him. So I fed him music.

"Tell me more about Beethoven, Mutti," he would ask, or "Could we hear the *Archduke Trio* again?"

I adored him and enjoyed his company as if he were a good friend. He was very responsible, trustworthy, obedient. Such a winsome child. How blessed we were. To be truthful, I was sad to have him leave home to start school.

Once there, he did well, soon reading beyond his grade level and independently at home. Both Paul and I had attempted to give him stimulating experiences to excite his imagination and curiosity, but we shied away from teaching at home the subjects that were part of the school curriculum, like arithmetic and reading. One day I picked up one of his books and found a marker on page 71.

"Tell me where this book came from," I asked.

"Oh, Heinrich loaned it to me."

Heinrich was a year or so older than Fritzi. They were friends because they walked to school together.

"Why is this bookmark in the book?"

"Because that's where I stopped reading."

I knew that we hadn't taught him to read, but I humored the boy.

"Please read page 70 for me."

It was an advanced reader with several paragraphs on a page. He read the whole page right off.

"Where did you learn all the words?" I wanted to know.

"Well, since you wouldn't teach me to read, I just had to teach myself."

As long as he didn't start reading the newspapers loaded with propaganda, I was pleased with his enthusiasm except for one unquenchable passion: motorcycles! The SS officers in town roared through the streets with their heavy vehicles. Usually we didn't see them before we heard them revving up before speeding by, sitting stiffly and proudly like gods on magic steeds. Some days I noted quite a few soldiers in town.

Seeing them kept us aware that Germany was at war, even though our town in Silesia was quite removed from fighting. We heard on the limited radio broadcasts available to us that all was going well for the Nazis. I looked away from the large posters of Hitler with his right arm raised in that well-known salute. Paul's classes contained fewer and fewer young men as they were conscripted, but his research continued unimpeded. Fritzi, fortunately, was too young to be forced into any youth corps.

I trusted that in time the war would be over out there--in England, in France, in Italy, in the Netherlands, in southern Germany, in every place Hitler infected with fascism. The "front" was far away. We suffered no air strikes. We never considered losing the war or its consequences, but at the same time, we didn't want to live in a totalitarian state under Hitler. A report in October 1941 boasted that Germany had three million Soviet prisoners in the few months since Hitler invaded Russia.

Unfortunately too many people had their passions fueled to patriotic white heat. Propaganda was uncensored. The Nazi party and the SS and the local police were no longer to be considered of little consequence. They had too many true believers. Fields were fertile for sprouting fanaticism. People like us learned to keep our political opinions to ourselves.

Time allowing, I read my favorite authors, to myself and to Fritzi. When he was small, he didn't know what I was reading, but he liked snuggling against me and listening to my voice. In bad weather, we played simple games. On nice days, we would walk to the pond to feed ducks and laugh over their competition for our crumbs. Or he sailed little wooden boats on strings.

As we sauntered, I told him stories he wanted to hear over and over again. Jason's search for the golden fleece, Odysseus' recruitment for the Trojan War, Sisyphus' eternal task, Narcissus' captivation by his reflection, and others.

I was delighted to share my love of literature with Fritzi. One course in the subject I shall never forget because of Professor Stark. My first sight of the old man was when he entered the lecture hall. Walking with two canes and grasping a sheaf of papers, he shuffled to the lectern.

We knew the routine: the old man would first put down his notes, raise and then scrunch his busy white eyebrows above those sharp, dark eyes, run his hands back to tame the wild white hair that didn't seem ever to have seen a barber. At the sound of the bell to begin class, he started to talk.

Taking notes was easy for us because he spoke slowly and clearly. From time to time, he would stop to ask a random question of someone. A student who had not been paying strict attention was a sure target. Faltering or giving a wrong answer was unforgivable. Usually Professor Stark would then lean forward and shout obscenities. On days when he was more energetic, he responded to a wrong answer by marching around the room, throwing up his hands and calling upon every god and goddess known to the Greeks to set the world right again. Insulted and publicly disgraced, the chastised student made sure that he would never so suffer again. On the other hand, witty remarks brought smiles to our faces and endeared the octogenarian to us. When he quoted Friedrich Schiller as a researcher of imagination and vision, he became almost ecstatic with adulation. We knew that there would not be many more years for students to benefit from someone so wedded to his subject.

Fritzi's relationship with his father was different from his with me. Paul wasn't the playful type. His character was dry, reserved, formal. Our son didn't fear his father at all, but he knew his Vati demanded respect. They would sit together after supper to review Fritzi's schoolwork while I washed up and mended. I could easily have helped with the school lessons but felt that father-son bonding took precedence. I knew my place and myself.

DECEMBER 1944

"Just look at Fritzi," Paul said in a voice heavy with sorrow. "What choices will he have as he grows into manhood? In too few years he'll be conscripted into the Hitler Youth and then blindly march into a dark future as a soldier or as a policeman."

I didn't bury my head in the sand regarding the political situation, but on the other hand I had to spend much time each week planning our meals and stretching the food budget. Milk and eggs were becoming scarce; for several years ration cards had restricted my buying even when certain foods were available, but now the cards permitted even less. If I used carrots and potatoes from the basement, could I afford boiled beef with horseradish tomorrow? Homegrown onions and wilted beets might accompany my favorite noodles and veal strips with apple *kuchen* for dessert, with just a pinch of sugar. Paul often asked for veal cutlets and sausages with fried potatoes.

"I must let you know at once," he instructed early in our marriage, "there is one food which I shall never eat. I like pureed potatoes but not with caraway seeds. I find it impossible to separate the seeds from the puree while eating."

It wasn't a problem. I'd never heard of the combination.

Prices were rising weekly on all foodstuffs. In the fall Fritzi had helped me gather wild blackberries near the forest and even helped to make preserves. The jars sat on shelves in the basement along with apples from our own tree. My mother had taught me how to preserve fruits and vegetables, so I could easily feed my husband's body, but providing his soul with nourishment was more difficult.

I don't think we were a "close" couple who celebrated wedding anniversaries, shared a special song, or had birthday parties, except those for Fritzi. We loaded all our love onto him. Ours wasn't a marriage of convenience, or was it?

I led the domestic life. Away from the lab for years now, I didn't know how few students remained nor was I privy to the content of guarded conversations among the faculty. Paul didn't bring home the details. The tenor of our life together had been calm. There was little laughter. Romance? No. That chapter had been omitted from my life book. How could I find it now, living with a man seized by fear, obsessed by the Nazi demons? And memories of Hermann haunted me.

Paul usually became quiet when Fritzi came with his schoolbooks into the kitchen. We were spending most of our time back there in order to economize. The stove was a sort of stove-fireplace that warmed the room. Fuel was scarce, and heating other rooms too expensive.

On cold nights we were quite cozy there because the room was large enough to accommodate the sofa we had moved from the living room. Life was becoming more harsh, but each day I lifted the stiff lace curtains of the parlor to tend a geranium plant in the window, giving it food and water with the hope of putting flowers back into our lives.

Now, so many years away from those days, Paul's face comes back to me as if we were still sitting at the kitchen table. Wrinkles of worry began to darken his handsome face. Surely after defeats in Russia and North Africa Hitler's war was lost. The entry of the United States and strength of the Allies should have sent him a positive message. He had begun to gradually withdraw our savings, the few that we had, from the bank.

"I can't predict what the future holds, what demands Hitler may make on his already impoverished people, but we may need cash in an emergency."

A few critical voices were rising above quiet murmurings, but too few and always in private. Many were convinced Nazi Germany would be defeated. Others maintained our nation would return to the glory it deserved, that the sacrifices by death and the hardships of war would be avenged. Rumors ran rampant with reports of last-minute miracle weapons. Throughout the town a new police force and SS troops dominated every square.

We often heard Goebbels on the radio, proclaiming victories for the Germans and foreseeing an early end to the war. Where we lived in eastern Germany, Silesia, the war seemed far away. The distance to the battles was considerable; we experienced no air strikes. In spite of some shortages and restrictions and the military, I felt a tentative security.

"Our father in heaven. Be merciful in your judgment." Paul repeated this prayer daily. He would stare long into my eyes. Did he read fear or trust? He never asked.

"Oh, Paul, Hitler WILL be defeated," I obstinately responded. "He's the epitome of evil, the devil in person."

I put up a brave front. I had lived in this town for the past 16 years, in this country, my Heimat [homeland], for my entire life.

". . . . Be merciful in your judgment." Who was being judged? Was this the result of "Thy will be done"? We were innocent. Our leaders were the criminals. But would we perish in the final annihilation? Or perish in the severe winter from lack of fuel? We couldn't guess what was to come.

1945

JANUARY

The migration of refugees from east to west began as a trickle, barely noticed.

Die Russen kommen! ("The Russians are coming!")

The first refugees were the wealthy, fleeing just days in front of the Russian push westward toward Berlin. In their cars they passed quickly through town; some even had drivers. A few autos broke down and had to be abandoned because we had no repair shops open. Townspeople scavenged them for parts. Those early refugees had *Reichmarks* to buy provisions at double the price along the way, depriving us as our stores ran out of food. Their extra cash took the place of rationing *Merken* (stamps.) Shopkeepers by this time cared more for money than regulations and eventually pulled down metal grates to the pavement and locked them for good.

Die Russen kommen!

More slowly, older cars came. Honking a path, they pushed forward as if through a herd of cows on a country road or a flock of sheep whose shepherd was lost. Horse-drawn wagons made their way among the cars, loaded so high that ropes held possessions piled a good one and a half meters above the side fences. Occasionally a small child crowned the load like an angel atop a Christmas tree.

Die Russen kommen!

The next flux was backpackers, fleeing on bicycles with extra packs on rear fenders. Children often rode on tricycles next to parents who walked, pushing wheelbarrows. Every imaginable type of vehicle had loads tied on the roof: wooden grocery crates, trunks, suitcases, even blankets sewn to make packing sacks. The initial slow trickles developed into a rushing stream, like the Rhine unloosed after heavy storms. Straw baskets hung from door handles, and people were oozing out the doors.

The slowest band was composed of people pulling handcarts, steeply loaded and with pots and pans hanging on the sides. Some had to be pulled by both the husband and wife. The weight of the load inhibited speed, but that pace was a blessing for the children, who usually dragged their weary little bodies alongside. I thought of the nomads in the desert, who packed up their belongings and migrated to new grazing grounds or markets, the children running alongside the camels. They owned and needed little. They weren't a flock of frightened individuals with torn clothing caked with mud, not knowing where they could sleep or when they would eat.

Die Russen kommen!

Quite a few in the moving crowd left the main road to find people like us, people who were staying put and might have something for them to eat. Several families came to our door, begging food to help carry them over a day or two or until they reached safety in the central Reich.

I always could find preserved fruit or vegetables for them, although since the daily open market was a memory we had been eating up our own inventory stored in the basement. Finally my compassion crumbled, and I was forced to turn them away empty handed, or I'd not answer their knocks. I had to keep some food for my own family.

During rainstorms the parade never slowed. Even carts covered with canvas became water logged. If an owner removed the tarp, his load was lighter but its contents were open to voracious paws. Evacuees often abandoned burdensome bundles. No one bothered to open them, to steal the discards of another. Each person was intent upon his or her own journey.

Like flotsam and jetsam, the human debris flowed along the asphalt road. Absolutely no organized evacuation plan existed. No German officials accompanied nor directed our destitute fellow citizens. The Nazis considered evacuees traitors unwilling to fight. Were these innocent people like us? We didn't know. Were they party members? We didn't know. Were they Nazis in fear for their lives? We didn't know, and we didn't ask. Undoubtedly many were affiliated with the Nazis in some way and frightened at the thought of repercussions. Eventually the local streets emptied except for people scrounging for food and those of us who stayed behind.

2 FEBRUARY | FRIDAY

One day the police recruited Paul to work at the main railway station. There he found an overwhelming mass of piled suitcases, packing cases, trunks, and even burlap bags with tags. He told me, "People were sleeping all over the floor inside the station. Outside they stood in the slush. They propped their heads on worn leather suitcases or wooden boxes because no one cared to be away from his precious goods."

"Probably those things wouldn't have much value for anyone else."

"The tragedy is that no trains are running and may not run for days or ever. I felt very sorry for people with children. Little ones screamed; older ones cried."

"The poor souls. How long will it be before their hope turns to despair?"

"When that happens, they will have to abandon those heavy boxes and cases. It is a miracle they got them as far as the station. One scene was particularly pathetic."

"Tell me, Paul."

"A man, rather well dressed in a dark suit and wearing a tie, had opened his suitcase and was trying to sell some of his possessions."

"Ach, what a pity. I doubt that he had customers."

"You are right! And I heard that quite a few cars had broken down outside town. People had to abandon them and continue on foot or come to the station. You can guess what happened next."

"Looters, of course, and probably some of our own people from here in Liegenbruck. "

"Not only did gangs carry away loaded containers, but they were stealing tires off the cars and disemboweling the engines."

"Oh, Paul, what is this country coming to?"

"I have been telling you about people I don't know and have never seen before. Now listen to this. There we were toiling in the slushy snow, our arms aching so that we could hardly lift another kilo. And who was standing there, watching? That blackguard Baumgartner. That lawless lawyer just stood there like some haughty supervisor, not daring to spot his immaculate spats, not wanting to wrinkle or dampen his sharply creased trousers. What an anachronism of his entire profession! I am sure he considered himself a better-class German, too important for a humanitarian chore. And do you know what he said? He kept repeating, 'Crushing. Crushing.'"

I interrupted, "You know he's a Party member and that his wife is a leader in the women's corps."

"Yes, I know, but he could have lifted a hand. I wished I could 'crush' him. Those were his countrymen who needed help. And do you know who else was there? Neumann. My old colleague Neumann. You can't imagine the bile that rose in me when I spotted him in full battle dress, so proudly flaunting his uniform as he tried to keep order in that melee. Children's sobs filled the air. Mothers were wailing as they tried to pacify their little ones. Some men, maybe fathers, maybe not, were wandering around. I've never heard such foul language as theirs."

The two of us had become accustomed to talking in almost whispers, even in our own home, trying to protect Fritzi from the outside activities. Of course, he could hear almost constantly the Russian artillery barrage. He stopped hiding at the sound, but it was still frightful for him.

"So help me, Hannah. I could not help myself. I went up to Neumann and asked him if he wasn't eager to flee with his family, like those refugees on the train. I reminded him that the Russians would not overlook his past record. 'You should look out for yourself,' I goaded. Truly, I do not believe the man was aware of my derision. He straightened his back, stuck out his chest, was determined to stay till the end.

"If worse comes to worst," he boasted, "the Party's district governor has reserved a place for me in the official car."

"I could not resist continuing, 'I would not let myself be deluded that the governor will really keep his word.' Neumann stiffened."

"Oh, Paul," I warned. "You mustn't bait someone so powerful, even if you two were once colleagues at the university. Think of what might happen to Fritzi and me if you are taken away."

"No fear. He did not have a chance to protest, nor did I continue. Just then a whole crowd pushed against him."

As it turned out, the following day Baumgartner chose the better part of valor and fled with his family. A few days later Neumann waited in vain for the governor's car. At least 80% of the citizens of Liegenbruck were seized by the manic panic and left. Even Paul's friends who swore they would stay decided to flee. Some were Party members. Constantly booming cannons from the east forced the hordes westward. The engulfing power of the Russians invaders was upon us.

5 FEBRUARY | MONDAY

Autumn leaves had long been gone and most birds with them. I needed to buy more food during the winter than when I raised our own vegetables, and I often became impatient waiting for the ground to defrost. In the fall, I dug root crops to store in the basement. All of the flats in our building had two floors, a garden space, and a shared common basement with locked gates separating each family's compartment from the next. Our space was ample. Down there I was always reminded of a poem I learned at the gymnasium. It was by the American Robert Frost and said "good fences make good neighbors." He was right.

Since Fritzi's school had been closed, I taught him a few English poems at home as well as having him keep up with math and writing. Getting him to read had never been a problem. He was loving and intelligent and rather healthy considering what nutrition was available.

I grieved for my fellow citizens in flight and tried to cheer myself by considering my own good fortune. Paul was too old for conscription. He did not fall in the crushing of Italy. He was not taken a prisoner in the Balkans. He had been a faithful husband and a good provider, and warmer weather was on its way.

Bulbs in our little garden would sprout and spread cheer with their bonny blooms. Blossoms would appear and fall from the apple tree, and we would wait for the fruit to turn eventually from green to gold.

I longed to have the windows open to the sweet air of spring and to walk in the forest. After warm rains, I could look for mushrooms. My eyes were well trained from childhood to distinguish the good ones from the poisonous ones. Oh, a plate of mushrooms fried in butter! Well, perhaps not butter considering the strict rationing, but mushrooms, at least.

Like nature, good would prevail, even though I knew that flowers fade and fruit rots and green leaves crisp and fall. The war was not over, and spring had not yet come.

In the east and west our "leaders" failed. Radio reception had been shut off, but all we had been getting anyway was military music. Should we leave our home here on the eastern frontier for the interior? The Russians were on their way. but what did we have to fear from them? We were not the military. We were not party members. We reasoned that the Russians would quickly pass through the town, that we citizens would offer no resistance, and that life would be very much as it was.

Fritzi was nearly eight. We could still eat, though not nearly as well as before. Meat was scarce, and we could have a small amount only every second or third day. We continued our self-imposed censorship. How dare we air our opinions in the streets? A word dropped here, a phrase there . . . . ach, I wouldn't think about it.

That fear of treason was constantly on my mind because there was no defense against a charge, and some German officials were still in town. But to be realistic, by that time very few people remained to denounce us. Still, we locked the doors to our flat and spent quiet evenings engrossed in our readings or tutoring Fritzi. His friend Heinrich was gone. I endlessly read him poems; he never tired of Uhland's rhythmic "Song of the Mountain Shepherd Boy."

> *"Ich bin vom Berg der Hirtenknab',*
> *Seh'auf die Schlösser all herab;*
> *Die Sonne strahlt am ersten hier,*
> *Am längsten weilet sie bei mir;*
> *Ich bin der Knab'vom Berge!"*

> *"I am the shepherd boy from the mountain,*
> *the castle lies below me,*
> *the sun shines earliest here*
> *[and] stays with me the longest,*
> *I am the boy from the mountains."*
> *He drinks from the gushing stream, is cheerful*
> *in tempests and thunder storms until he has to*
> *join the throng below because of a forest fire.*

While listening, Fritzi always held his favorite possession, a canteen, and sipped from it, pretending he too was in the mountains. If it was a windy, stormy day, the poem gave him courage, and I recall when he was much younger, he said: "Close the window and let the wind play outside all by itself." He made his own breezes by using the old swing under our plum tree, nowadays a safe outdoor activity. I didn't like for him to be out on the streets by himself, so Paul and I would take him on carefully planned walks.

Only occasionally did Paul visit his lab. His pessimism seemed to have infected his quest for new formulae and killed any enthusiasm for work there. One day he came home and began a familiar speech I knew so well: "Hannah, we have to talk seriously. I am torn with such turmoil. One part of me warns that we should leave Germany. The other part says that this is the only life we know. Most of my former colleagues have left. Only two residents in our block remain. The town is an empty shell, and the Russians have taken over the eastern part of the city."

I was distraught, having heard all this before.

"Do you mean we should leave town now? How can we go on the road with our little boy? There's no transport out of here. Are we to freeze on the road? And now there's no one left even to bury us."

Years before I had left this decision to him. We might easily have moved then, but this was not the time to remind him.

"Ach, mein Gott, you are right, Hannah."

He was silent most of the evening, deep in thoughts he had no inclination to share, and I didn't press him.

The university buildings closed down completely a day later. Paul was commanded to instruct at the temporary air force base. Heaven only knows what he could teach pilots, and we never talked about his teaching there.

He was grateful that at this Luftwaffe post he could closely observe first hand the tension of the Nazis' hopelessness. At least he'd found a friend in the battery chef Schoenherr. With him he could talk about Fritzi and condemn the brutality of the Nazis. His new companion didn't damn the military failure, but he damned the criminal foundation of the entire Nazi political machine. That work at the base lasted less than week, and Paul worried anew.

"The Russians are between here and the airport, so now I have no way to communicate with Schoenherr for help. Besides, I agonize every day and every night over being so desperate for a friend that I revealed my thoughts to him. What if he denounces me?"

I counseled that rather than worry about the danger of being denounced he should worry about the danger of our being alone in a house on a nearly abandoned street. Quite soon, on a cold February day, the rest of Liegenbruck fell.

Nervous officials at the base had planned to blow up all the buildings: the barracks, the mill, the commissary. The situation was drastic. Finally the commandant, in a humanitarian moment, ordered removal of the fuse line to the bomb. He realized that horrendous destruction would not fall upon the invading Russians but upon the German population itself.

The Russians came in. Deafening thud thud thuds were all we could hear. We knew that those sounds were the barrage of cannons and explosives and gunfire. Armed vehicles, their motors roaring, were the first to clatter on the street outside. Next tanks pounded the cobblestones. The lights at the front of them stared forward like the eyes of a giant armored beast. Two soldiers sat atop on each side of the enormous protruding gun. Each soldier had his own gun, which he kept aiming in all directions and shooting into the air to send us scurrying. We hurried inside to find the windows of our flat rattling as if suffering an earthquake. The machine guns scared Fritzi, and he cried almost all the time. We stayed inside and stood back to avoid being seen. I was consciously frightened nearly to paralysis during the day, and at night my unconscious brought more nightmares.

In spite of his pessimism, Paul convinced himself the Russians would quickly realize the civilian population which remained in town posed no threat. Then they would march westward after establishing a temporary government of sorts. The Russian occupation aroused mixed feelings. Those of us who didn't belong to the Party already felt the town had been occupied, not by an outside enemy but by enemies within, the police and the SS. They hadn't menaced us with weapons of war but in a more sinister way, seeking citizens to betray or lie about each other.

8 FEBRUARY | THURSDAY

We had no premonition of what was to come with the new occupation. One day the Russians rounded up a small army of German men, some more able than others, for a special duty. I didn't know that and was worried when Paul didn't come home at midday from his morning walk nor later while the sky was still slightly light. I sensed danger in the dusk. At last he arrived, and I asked in a quivering voice, "Where have you been?"

I grasped him and clung to him before he could take off his overcoat. Never before had I seen his face so careworn.

"Hannah, I could not tell you I would be away."

He followed me into the kitchen, not even removing his wet shoes. I could see that his trousers were soaking wet. At first he couldn't talk, gazing toward Fritzi, who was sitting on the couch with Grimm's *Fairy Tales.*

"It's time to get ready for bed now. I'll be upstairs soon to tell you good night. Your father is very tired. I want to talk to him for a while."

Perplexed, Fritzi obediently left us. He was a quiet boy, tall and thin for his age, possessed of his father's heavy shock of blond hair. But it tore at my heart to look at that innocent child. His eyes expressed varying degrees of fear and bafflement. His childhood was disintegrating more each day as his trust in all he had ever known was eroding. And how quickly he was outgrowing his clothes, with nothing to replace them.

Although Paul sat down at the table, he made no effort to taste the bread and wurst, which he pushed aside. His head dropped forward, and he trembled as tears rushed from his swollen eyes. I had never seen my husband cry before except when I told him I was pregnant. Those were tears of joy. He ran his fingers over and over through his thick hair, then grasped his head on both sides in grief.

"Ach, I had decided to go to the university, feeling somewhat better about the situation. I still had the keys to the building and to my lab. A few others had gotten in to work, too. I was cleaning some test tubes when Wiltfang barged in and demanded I stop whatever I was doing and dress for work. I told him I was at work, as well he knew."

"*Guten Himmel*, Paul. What had you done or said?"

"Nothing. Absolutely nothing."

"You look exhausted. It's been dark for hours. Where have you been?"

He continued. "I then noticed that a Russian soldier was behind Wiltfong. In quite broken German he made me understand I was to get my overcoat and gloves. I complied and followed him to the front of the main science building. Already waiting there were three of my colleagues--Klaus Wagner, Fritz Kuntz, and Heinrich Salwasser--and a few other people I didn't know.

They commandeered us into a row. Anyone who was slow received a blow on his side with a rifle. Thanks be to the good Lord that I'm strong for my years. We had to march only about 2K to the old road toward Kurzfeld and then turned left in the direction of Metzafor. Along the way more soldiers began to lead us to where a small crowd had been assembled and was busy digging a ditch."

"Surely the Russians don't expect the Germans to turn back for a counter attack," I interjected.

"No, Hannah. It was not a trench they were digging but a mass grave. Twelve bodies lay piled beside the road. All women and children. All dead and frozen stiff. Some might even have been those refugees who came to our door begging food."

"What horror! Our little food for them probably gave them only a single day more of living. It's inhumane! But, Paul, if you started early in the morning, why are you so late?"

"In addition, the Russians wanted us to remove gold wedding bands and boots. Just imagine! It was impossible with frozen bodies."

"That's absolutely savage."

"After burying those bodies, we were forced to walk further along the road. A large contingent of conscripts from town came with shovels, so our small group became a crowd. They split us into units as we went along.

"The first unit stopped at a large pile of bodies and had to start digging again. The rest of us went on to see another pile of bodies. All dead refugees, so a second unit stayed behind to dig. Each time we stopped, a soldier counted off workers. Those savage Russians had earlier gone along the road, throwing off a determined number of bodies like gunny sacks of grain left at a farmer's gate. I was quickly numbed at the sight of so many dead civilians. More and more and more! We counted 243, mostly women and children. Two hundred forty three!

"Digging into the frozen ground was nearly impossible, like breaking into rocks, so the graves, of course, were shallow. As we neared the Lutheran cemetery of the Good Pastor, we persuaded the Russians to let us take some bodies in there. You know the place. Finally it became too dark to see what we were doing, so the Russians marched us back into town."

"Paul, we still see occasional refugees straggling through our streets. They don't have baggage and believe they're headed for safety. The poor wretches!"

"Our father in heaven, please make those dense blond Nazi blockheads aware of the destruction they have wrought. So much for our government. Our own German officials couldn't even provide shelter or transport for those miserable souls, whoever they were."

"Paul, you haven't had anything to eat all day."

"Had they given us something, I could not have taken it."

I couldn't eat either and noticed I had unconsciously made a pile of crumbs from my brown bread. We slowly made our way to bed, overcome by despair.

9 FEBRUARY | FRIDAY

In the midst of our troubled sleep that night we heard a horrendous boom that could come only from a bomb exploding. Both Paul and I were frightened but jumped from our bed and ran to the window looking down at our front entrance. We saw flames a few houses away and wires lying in the street, exposed and crackling like thunder in broken streaks of lightning. It was as if a violent storm had plunged downward from the sky to wreak its vengeance atop the earth. Smaller explosions from the fallen wires menacingly leaped closer and closer.

"Hurry, Hannah. We must get to a shelter at once. Get Fritzi!"

It wasn't necessary to wake him, for he was out of his bed and running to our room.

"Mutti, Mutti," he screamed. "What's happening?"

Without taking time to comfort the trembling child, I told him to get on shoes and his warm coat as quickly as possible and to wait for us at the front door. I grabbed a blanket as I fled the bedroom. Beneath a smoking red sky we rushed away from the blaze.

Fritzi anxiously gripped my hand, screaming as blasts increased in intensity. On adjacent streets burning buildings blocked escape. The entire neighborhood seemed to be afire. Although the street lights were out, the flames brightened the sky like daylight.

Already we could see there would be no home left for the Lempkes and the Kobernas. We finally reached the shelter, which wasn't as crowded as I had expected because so many in the area had gone away. Had I known we'd arrive there safely, I would have grabbed at least a second blanket.

"Oh, Paul! What if we have no house waiting for us when we come out? I can't bear the thought!"

He was silent. What was he to say? Tortured by the fact he had kept his family with him so long, he could no longer find justification. At once I was ridden with guilt. What was I saying? Worrying about the house and lost possessions. I should think before blurting out my thoughts. Didn't Paul suffer enough?

He asked, "Can you guess my thoughts?"

"Forget your thoughts for now. Tomorrow everything will be over. The front line won't be here any more, and we can return to a normal life. Let's try to rest now."

Our little family got no sleep that night, kept awake by the dampness and cold, by the relentless bombardment outside. The experience was like living a nightmare, worsened by the toxic odor of fear in the shelter. Daybreak brought silence above, but below Paul was not to be deterred from punishing himself.

"Oh, Hannah, I have failed you two. I made all my decisions to the best of my knowledge and in good conscience. Now I feel like Job, a defeated man."

As I saw Paul begin to crumble, some new courage was surging through me.

"Come, come, Paul. Enough of that! Let's go outside to see what's left of our neighborhood."

The sky was so black, in spite of its being daylight, that we could hardly see where to go. Breathing was difficult, and I wanted to proceed with eyes closed to stop their burning. At one point the air seemed clearer, and I could see red flames surrounded by an orange ring whose center was black swirling smoke. Had I not known what was happening, I'd have stood in awe of the beautiful forms.

A stale, charred odor permeated the air beneath tents of smoke that shaded smoldering timbers. Where walls remained, their plaster often didn't. Stucco piles lay at the foundations of houses, where often a few uprights of the frame gasped their last, still smoking. We pushed our stiff limbs through deserted streets and praised the Lord upon finding our house intact. Only later did we learn that in certain areas where the fires hadn't entirely destroyed buildings, the Russians returned with fuel to reignite the remains. Had we known, we might not so confidently have reclaimed our former sanctuary.

"We shall go upstairs and crawl into bed," Paul directed, having regained his composure.

"We need rest and warmth. You probably feel as numb as I do," I replied in support.

"Mutti, may I sleep with you and Vati? I'm so afraid to be alone."

Of course we took him into our bed between us and even succumbed to slumber for several hours.

Upon awakening, we looked down again onto the street to see German soldiers running in all directions with no apparent purpose in their movements. Nevertheless, they gave us a sense of safety, so we three crawled back into bed. Somewhat later, Paul looked out again and reported the street was empty. But not for long. We heard the revving of engines and clanging metal. The pavement was filled this time with Russian soldiers carrying machine guns and accompanied by armored cars and cannons.

"Come look, Hannah," Paul whispered, for Fritzi was finally sleeping. "Our father in heaven. Thy will be done."

Fritzi's slumber was soon shattered by the crackling of small arms. Hundreds of Russian soldiers were running and scattered like ants from a disturbed nest. Each carried a gun and shot into the air. More and more and more and more passed by. The city was completely in enemy hands. They didn't seem to be looking for people or checking houses but simply creating an atmosphere of fear.

Earlier, when Paul foresaw the possibility of having no water, gas, or electricity, we began preparations for the inevitable. Our town had many ponds, natural and man-made, strategically located for providing water to douse neighborhood fires. Paul had filled the bathtub, five liters at a time, from the suspended tank and procured a kerosene lamp and fuel. If deprived, we would at least have drinking water and fuel for cooking. Two burner plates on the kitchen stove could be heated with scraps from the wood pile. We sequestered ourselves, not daring even to venture into the yard, but Paul was confident that we soon would be able to resume normal life.

It had been eight days since the mass exodus from Liegenbruck began. Though noises from outside were disquieting, one afternoon I daringly took a bucket to the pond to fetch water for washing. I really wanted to find out whether the soldiers would stop me, but I was just a hausfrau. The trip was uneventful. A few Russian soldiers in the street ignored me. I felt relaxed about our situation until later in the day when the cacophony resumed. Tanks were overturning fences and trees, accompanied by shots and bursting hand grenades. What more could the Russians do? They had our town.

12 FEBRUARY | MONDAY

We were terrified when loud knocks came a few days later to our front door, not made with closed fists but with blunt gun handles.

"Where are the residents from this sector?" asked one of the four Russian officers as they pushed their way into the hall. Their manners were no different from those of the Germans who wore swastikas.

"Gone, they are all gone," Paul told them. He didn't consider it necessary to mention that another family lived nearby.

"Only my wife and my little boy and I are left here. He's nearly eight."

Fritzi and I had accompanied Paul to the door. They could see that we were all there, but they didn't believe him and continued forcing their way past us inside, weapons ready. Two methodically went down the hall, peering into the living room on the way, while the other two went upstairs, pointing their guns ahead. We waited at the front door, not knowing what to expect next. Once they saw my husband had told the truth, they became quite polite and patted Fritzi's head. They were full of questions.

"Why have all the people left?"

"Where have they gone?"

"Were they Party members?"

"When did they leave?"

Paul patiently replied that propaganda had frightened them. Many were Party members with maimed consciences. At last he was able to express openly his antagonism toward the Nazis.

Thus warmed up, the officers became more genial and wanted schnapps.

"Here, gentlemen, is the last of my German brandy and a fine Rhine wine."

"Ah ha, this is what we need!"

The Russian officers stayed for quite a while, inquiring about us and why we had stayed behind. All were young, about 20 to 25, and obviously educated. Their German had rather the accent of speakers from Berlin, indicating that it was learned in school and not on the streets.

Paul explained his antagonism. "Since we had no use for the Nazis and saw the Russian front advancing, we felt safer staying at home. But years ago, when my wife became pregnant and many people left Germany, it did not seem wise for us to leave, considering my age and her condition."

I thought to myself, "These soldiers, though they speak our language to some extent, may have limited vocabularies, and I wonder how much of what Paul was telling them they really understood. It's one thing to make demands and ask simple questions in a foreign tongue, but to understand the answers or Paul's erudite explanations was another thing.

Their leader was called Igor by the others as they conversed among themselves in their own language. Fritzi was fascinated by the foreign sounds because he had never heard anything but German spoken. Igor was quite handsome, having high cheek bones and dark hair. His hazel eyes seemed honest, and I could relate to these young fellows as human beings doing their duty in wartime. At length, one said,

"Herr Merkel, *Kommen Sie mit uns.* (Come with us. We give rations.) *Sie muss nicht hungrig gehen.* (You must not go hungry.) Perhaps you no get food if alone."

How I trembled to see Paul leave the house with those armed men. I suddenly didn't trust their politeness, their promise of food.

"Where are they taking Vati?" cried Fritzi.

Would I soon be a widow? Oh, God in heaven, do we deserve this?

Sooner than I could have hoped, Paul returned with only one officer.

"Look, Hannah. Flour, sugar, noodles, and so much more. They wanted to give me more than I could carry so Igor came along to help me."

Igor didn't stay this time but left after he had carried the food to the kitchen. Later Paul confessed,

"I am rather troubled and have such mixed feelings. All this food is from a German warehouse."

"But you couldn't refuse."

"No you are right. I hope I can share this with some other Germans when they turn up."

The next day came another knock on the door, this time a firm hand knock. Paul confidently opened it to see Igor with a brand-new woman's bicycle.

"For your son!"

Conscience-ridden with divided loyalties, Paul graciously accepted it, recognizing it as belonging to Frau Knockl, who had left town. Igor left at once.

Paul later returned it, undamaged, to the house where it belonged. In a tight neighborhood like ours, everyone was aware of each other's property. To anyone who remained, the appearance of the new bicycle could not go unnoticed. Though the owners were gone, Paul was sure they soon would return.

"Hannah, we are over the mountain. Things cannot be so bad anymore."

How profoundly Paul deceived himself, or did he? Was he simply putting on a brave front for Fritzi and me? A man so prone to pessimism! Could he change so quickly? Or was he disguising his fear with optimistic phrases?

13-17 FEBRUARY
TUESDAY TO SATURDAY

Unfortunately Paul's sunny attitude began to darken as clouds brought cold rain. It mercifully quenched small fires still smoldering and erased our fears of new fires starting from flying embers. Beginning that day and on the following days more Russian soldiers came to our door, five or six at a time, often with no officer. They were not the friendly group who made the first visit but a gang of street bullies out of control. They *blitzkrieged* our house, savagely upsetting furniture and larders in search of hidden weapons and Nazi soldiers. One thing after another disappeared each time the soldiers visited. The robberies at first were comparatively small: drawers and door handles. The next time it was jewelry, the little I had, and photographic equipment. I winced when warm clothing, primarily jackets and my high boots, were confiscated, followed by most of our socks. I've always kept our home in order, so this commotion and upheaval were unnerving.

Never did we expect the Russians to take such advantage of us. We assumed they would enter the town, find no resistance and advance in the direction of Berlin.

But our own disorder was nothing. The looters wildly invaded the empty houses nearby if they hadn't been burned to the ground. They tossed household furnishings out of smashed windows and doors. Tables, chairs, and upholstered furniture lay broken in muddy yards.

The marauders loaded trucks, mainly with clothing and household goods, piling mattresses over all. Gangs of young toughs in uniform trampled linens, which had been thrown into the streets. Then wind blasts coupled with rain, so common at that time of year, drenched the sheets and tablecloths, plastering them to the ground with sooty sludge.

I was stunned at such senseless mayhem. It was through this very street that for many years local bands used to march and play old familiar songs. Those memories were almost erased when later *Deutschland uber Alles* replaced those songs and when flags with swastikas waved instead of local banners. And now this rubble!

It was hard to face the fact honestly that our troops on Russian soil would have been no different. Some of these pillaging soldiers probably had experienced the same thing in their villages, rape of their women, burning of their homes, and random shootings of the innocent. They'd been storing up hatred for us. Now they unleashed it.

Dear Paul, whose lab was always a paradigm of organization, dug those dirty linens from the street and piled them neatly on the ground, intending to wash them when convenient, thinking our former neighbors would be thankful for the remnants he could   save.

While he was busy with this task, three fellow townsmen approached him, out exploring to see who was left. He said they compared experiences and that some had suffered horrendously. All of them were thankful to have survived the first four days.

"I joined them to check out the town. It's even worse than it is here."

"How can that be?" I asked.

"All the stores are empty and plundered. Buildings have been reduced to cinders. Every sort of litter surrounds abandoned houses. I'm so happy to be back here with you and Fritzi. Soon these Russians will have to go on and leave us in peace."

How wrong he was! The next morning while he was taking a walk, soldiers grabbed him for forced labor. They held both his arms as they put him into a small jeep and drove to a local vocational school, where he became part of small team of other German men about his age. They had to clear a warehouse that had not been damaged, and evidently the looters had been warned away.

"My eyes nearly popped out," Paul told me. "So much material in the hands of the Russians. We loaded the best military fabric, but also peacetime articles. Wagon after wagon was piled high with loot. They even wanted shoes of all sizes, thousands of pairs. Luckily they were not guarding us too closely, so I slipped away. I knew you would be worried, and I hated to have you alone."

"To tell you the truth, I wasn't aware of how long you were away because I was so busy putting the house back together from the disruption by the last band of looters."

Then in a quiet voice, he whispered, "I have brought home Herr Hirsch, the owner of the iron works."

"But Paul," I protested. "We don't know him, and I've saved only enough of the midday hot meal for you."

"No, no. You do not understand. The Russians burst into his big house, throwing him out within five minutes. He was wandering helpless and homeless. I invited him to stay with us. It will be wise for us to have a second man in the house."

We didn't know the Hirsches, but I figured in times like this, we all should do what we can to help each other. I wasn't one to question Paul's judgment, and besides it was too late. From time to time I had seen Frau Hirsch in their car, driven by a chauffeur, or at a Stadtmusikchor performance. I loved to attend those concerts, and Paul told me he'd heard that not fifty years ago women would take along their knitting and drink beer while listening.

Herr Hirsch's wife was a middle-age woman with a matronly figure who wore gaudy clothing, though probably quite expensive. I imagine that her hair was graying and that she colored it because I had never seen hair so black, tightly permed. She powdered her flaccid cheeks heavily and wore very bright red lipstick the color of ripest strawberries. I always thought that she had stepped out of a painting by one of our German Expressionists.

"Thank you so very much, Frau Merkel, for joining your husband in taking pity on me."

"It's the least we can do for our fellow citizens in these trying times. Herr Hirsch, have you eaten?"

"Yes, thank you. I'm just fine in that respect."

I was looking at a man shorter than Paul, about my height, 5'10". His skin was very pale, but that could be due to the frightful experience he had just had. When he took off his dark brown hat, I saw that his hair also was brown, parted in the center and generously pomaded. It was heaviest above his ears. Small eyes, also brown, were deep set and contrasted strongly with full lips, the lower one especially puffed. His cheeks were full, too, and probably plain food hadn't passed through them for years. Beneath his business suit and vest he wore a starched shirt, dazzling in its whiteness. Paul's never were quite so bright in spite of drying in sunlight on good days. I'm sure his wife never spent considerable time turning the collars of his shirts to give them a second life, as I did when I was first married.

"Paul has just told me that the Russians evicted you from your home this morning."

"Yes, it was a dreadful experience, so unexpected."

"I don't want you to tire yourself repeating the story to me because you must be exhausted. Would you like to lie down to rest for a while?"

"I can't think of anything that would be better for me right now, if you don't mind."

I took him upstairs to Fritzi's room, which contained a spare double bed that had been Paul's when he was single. Once Herr Hirsch was settled, Paul ate his noon meal.

Both of us read for a while that afternoon, and Paul helped Fritzi with a jigsaw puzzle. The boy adored his father and giggled contentedly when they fitted a difficult shape. I wished Fritzi could get outdoors to play with another young boy in the neighborhood. He needed physical activity. It wasn't in Paul's nature to wrestle with his son on the floor or to kick a ball back and forth. Boisterous play just wasn't in him, so Fritzi was quieter than most young fellows his age.

After his long nap Herr Hirsch joined us in the kitchen for supper. He looked better for having rested, but lamented the loss of his home. We didn't discuss what the next step would be in this situation because there was no planning for the future, let alone the rest of the day. I had never mingled with people like the Hirsches and was rather at a loss for a topic of conversation, but I needn't have worried for Herr Hirsch never stopped talking.

"We have such a beautiful parlor," he began. "The carpet has a pattern of intertwined roses, and a floral patterned paper with irises is on the walls. There's a large marble fireplace with two comfortable chairs with velvet seats in front of it, but having a fire there would cause smoke to stain the stone, so we don't use it. My wife loves decorating. She bought tucked velvet pillows with gold braid for the two velvet couches, but her pride is the fine china and glassware in the dining room cabinet that has glass doors to show it off. She chose Oriental lamps with silk shades that have the most delicate fringe. Our bookcases are filled with Oriental doodads and small figurines--you know how women like to collect.

"I cannot make myself think of Russians rabble inhabiting our house. I peeked into your parlor after my nap and saw a lot of books in your bookcase. We just don't have time to read."

Talking about his house seemed to relax him and he ardently proclaimed a mistake had been made and that he would be back in his luxurious mansion the next day. We politely listened. I thought of our sparsely furnished parlor with its plain plastered walls hung with a photo of Nietzsche and some reproductions of works by famous artists. I especially liked one of the Grand Canal in Venice by Canaletto. Next to an easy chair Paul had used for years was the bookcase he bought me as a wedding gift. He had some books in another case, but the majority of his library was in his office. I liked our parlor with my books and its sofa and pictures. If our parlor looked like his, I'd never want to go into it.

"I understand there can't be much time for reading when you're very busy with your factory. Your wife also must have activities that take her away from the house."

"Oh, yes, but she doesn't neglect the house. She has trained our servants to clean well. You won't find a water spot or speck of dust anywhere."

"We German women take pride in keeping an orderly house."

"Yes, you do. We recently made some expensive improvements to our house. You may have noticed in going past it that the glass in all the front windows was replaced with stronger panes and frames to keep out cold drafts."

Herr Hirsch tended to talk with his hands a great deal, almost like an Italian. I noticed they were soft and his fingernails were very clean and buffed. They hadn't known manual labor.

I was wearing a heavy tweed skirt, plain navy blouse, and a heavy sweater because we tried to accustom ourselves to lower temperatures in the house. Still it seems I was always asking Paul to bring in more wood for the stove. I assured our guest that his house must have been much warmer for the family this winter.

"Oh, yes it was. We also put up extra-heavy textured drapes, which tend to make a room seem warmer. I was pleased that in spite of those costs, I could afford a new touring car. My wife was able to load into it many of our possessions when she and the chauffeur left town a few weeks ago, but not with all that she wanted to take away. I stayed behind to take care of the factory."

Paul didn't have much to say as Herr Hirsch and I continued our apolitical conversation on neutral ground. I started to put some ham, bread, cheese and other foods on the table for our evening meal, thanks to Ivan's largesse. As I did so, Herr Hirsch continued with another story about remodeling their house:

"Four years ago we ordered a firm to make us new tiles for the roof. Summer was the best time to undertake the task, due to the weather. As soon as all materials were delivered, I gave them a check for 10,000 Reich marks, trusting that they would finish the work quite soon. But then we got disappointed terribly.

"The boss himself did not work at all with his men; he said he was suffering from a circulatory disturbance. We soon saw that none of his men were able to make a proper roof. I could not send them away since they had taken off the former roof, so we feared our house might be without a roof the whole winter. Not a single one of the men had mastered the task, and their foreman was already drunk when he arrived early in the morning. As we heard later, he had rented a pub somewhere, and was himself his best customer. The work was poorly done. I wrote the firm several letters to make the necessary repairs, but without any answer. Finally, after more than three months, I threatened to go to the courts. A couple of days later we got a letter from a barrister and a final bill. It was much too high, and the barrister demanded that we pay at once the whole amount; otherwise, we had to pay ten percent interest.

"Such charges are outrageous," I interjected.

"The judge ordered an expert to check the roof. This man came about half a year later, but both Frau Hirsch and I could see that he was obviously bribed. His opinion was that all had been well done. He didn't see that all tiles on the ridge were completely loose. So I demanded that he come himself to the court in order to explain everything he had written. During the proceedings, he even committed perjury twice, but I was able to disprove everything he had said. But what did the judge do? Although even a layman like me could tell that the expert was telling lies, the judge said that the expert was right and that I was the wrongdoer. More than that, he even threatened to arrest me for insulting the expert."

"Your story is incredible. It's hard to believe that an officer of the court could be so unfair."

"Finally I got a new judge when that judge left his post. I knew the new one because we used to play cards together. I won the case, but it took about four years. I think that the court must have feared that I would send copies of all documents to papers all over Germany and even to foreign papers like *The Los Angeles Times* and *The New York Times.*"

I don't believe I had ever met another person who talked, talked, talked for the sake of hearing his voice or trying to impress us with his wealth, even if he was head of a company. He reminded me of that obtuse policeman Hermann. At times he seemed out of touch with reality. Finally Paul, irritated by such crass materialism, got in a word to change the subject.

"Where has Frau Hirsch gone?"

"My wife took our two children with her when she left. I ordered her to get most of our money out of the bank and to fill suitcases with Dresden china, silver, jewelry, and whatever else she thought of value. Emergency food and medicine. Oh, she wore her mink coat, of course."

Herr Hirsch was accustomed to a much more affluent lifestyle than ours. It wouldn't surprise me if he suffered gout. When our conversation finally edged on the present situation in Germany, he seemed unable to understand how the Reich had weakened, let alone how to come to terms with our country's present demise. Many of his employees at the factory had fled, so it became necessary to close down.

Paul and I were very circumspect in our comments but expressed surprise that as a Party member he had not left weeks ago. He remained clinging to his factory like a shipwrecked voyager to a wooden plank in twelve-foot waves or a captain who couldn't abandon his ship. Yet he knew the arrival of the Russians was imminent. At last, removing his gold-rimmed spectacles to rub his eyes, he asked to be excused for the evening.

He had exhausted both Paul and me. Fritzi hadn't said a word for hours, and we all retired. When we were by ourselves in bed, I asked: "How long is he going to be with us? What did you tell him?"

"It was all so sudden and unexpected that the subject never arose. He was very upset, really almost out of his mind. I had no alternative but to offer him assistance."

Needy or not, I found the man unbearable, completely lacking in humility, his present reality only fog. After spending the night and collecting his thoughts, thankfully he decided to leave us the next morning to regain possession of his house and, failing that, to search for his family. He was convinced once the Russian officers understood his importance, they would take all measures within their means to return his home to him or to give him safe passage westward. I doubt he was successful.

18-20 FEBRUARY
SUNDAY TO TUESDAY

It seemed Herr Hirsch had barely left when we heard another knock. Paul had dressed as usual in a suit with a tie as he always had while teaching. Perhaps in such attire he sensed a bit of his former dignity as we suffered indignities at the hands of our enemies.

Because we no longer had neighbors in the adjoining flat, I feared the knock meant a return of marauders. What more could they take? I shuddered as Paul went to see who it was.

Standing in the living room, out of sight but not out of earshot, I heard a young female voice pleading,

"Oh, good sir. Please help us! Please shelter us."

I didn't recognize the voice, but had a student come to us, she would have addressed Paul differently. He invited them in anyway. We didn't know whom to trust any more, let alone strangers. I began to question his judgment.

"Come, come in. Tell me what happened to you?"

When I came out, I understood. Two desperate girls were shaking and looked as if a bomb had exploded on them. What a sight!

They burst into tears. Neither looked older than 17 or 18. Bruised faces with bloody cuts just drying. No warm jackets. Torn, dirty blouses and skirts. Unkempt hair, stringy and tangled. Trembling with cold, the taller one began to explain, her body wracked with sobs. Before she could begin, she started to retch with dry heaves. I told them to follow me to the kitchen, where I gave them sips of warm water after they sat down.

"Russian soldiers came to our house. We live there with our father. He was away, conscripted for labor."

"Ah, well I understand," commented Paul.

"The soldiers said we were needed in their commissary--to prepare food."

The shorter sister interrupted, "They promised us safety and a safe return home. Of course, we had to go with them."

Both were so battered that it was difficult to distinguish a difference between them except by height. Looking around our modest kitchen, the only room with heat, they were aware we did not fare well, but they were not looking for an affluent family but just a house identifiable as having inhabitants.

"Please, please, let us hide here a day or two. We can't go into the street again to find our father, at least not right now."

The taller sister tried to stand up but fell to the floor. Paul helped her back to a chair. Fritzi began to cry, probably because he wasn't used to so many strangers in the house. I went to the couch to comfort him, leaving Paul to decide what we should do for the girls.

"Please, can you quietly explain to us what happened?"

The little blonde, at least she was once a golden-haired *Mädchen*, pushed back some strands of blood-caked hair from her hollow eyes. A rather bald patch on the top of her head showed that hair had been yanked out by the roots. She reminded me of the woman on the bridge in the famous painting *The Scream* by Edvard Munch. Speech was difficult due to a cut across her upper lip. Talking from the side of her mouth, she explained, "They didn't want us for kitchen work. They took us to an empty building on Gartenstrasse. We were thrown on the floor, had our skirts ripped and were raped."

"Good Lord in Heaven," I cried from across the room. "You poor children! The beasts!"

"Eight came for us." White-faced, she couldn't go on for a few moments, so convulsed was she with tremors. Then with tears and moans she continued, "Thirty or forty took us night and day for three days. We couldn't sleep. We wanted to die. We wanted to die. Sometimes we lost consciousness."

"Oh, may God have mercy on you! Of course you may stay with us." I made the decision.

"Give my husband your address, and perhaps he can find your father and bring him here to you. How did you get away?"

"Some officers came into the building and drove the creatures off, then picked us up and threw us outside onto a dirty pile of snow, like bags of potatoes."

Those ragged children undoubtedly were not the only objects of sexual rampages, yet we learned all women were not abused. Paul had heard of a woman on the next street. She was 54 years old and living in relative luxury. Regularly she sold herself and her daughter, 22, to the Russians. Paul assumed that others also profited from their bodies.

While I was appalled at the time, I wondered later if there might be some advantage in their controlling what was done to their bodies. Had they morally divorced themselves from the war? Veblen wrote about women as spoils of battle, trophies to be taken home. Centuries ago, in the *Iliad*, Homer told of Agamemnon's taking home Cassandra. Greek wives, waiting for their husbands' return from Troy, eagerly welcomed them back after the long absence. However, some, distraught because the men were accompanied by slave women trophies, found themselves abandoned and committed suicide. In certain societies families murder their violated daughters, who have disgraced them. Where will that mother and daughter be when the war ends? Do they care? Perhaps the only goal is staying alive another day in comfort and with food.

I hoped that I would be saved from having to make such decisions. Had our invading German soldiers treated the Russian women as those savages raped our young girls? Could a nation that gave the world Beethoven and Brahms and Goethe and Heine also produce raping beasts?

We tended their wounds as well as we could with our limited medical supplies. They needed sleep. From the kitchen I took them up a ladder into our loft overhead. It was the warmest place for the girls, and I had some extra blankets stored there. Fortunately the Russians had not taken any linens or bedding from us. In fact, they had ignored the loft in the turmoil of their searches. The girls climbed the ladder with difficulty, their mangled bodies barely able to endure the exertion.

Paul left with the hope of locating their father. While he was gone, Fritzi and I kept quiet in the kitchen, not wanting to disturb their rest. He loved poetry as much as I, so I turned to Liliencron's simple song *Die Musik Kommt* (*The Music Comes*) to take him away from our present situation. He always smiled as the King of Persia passes in triumph to the lyricist's opening lines: *Klingling, bumbum und tschingdada,* with meaning as clear in German as in English.

Several hours later Paul returned. Mission unaccomplished. The girls were awake, and I was able to persuade them to eat some cabbage soup after I mashed the vegetable to a gentle mush. They wanted nothing else but more sleep and to find their father.

Each time they stirred, I checked their wounds, not wanting infections to start, though who knows what kinds of venereal disease they probably had picked up. I often invited them down into the kitchen to eat whatever soft food I could prepare for them, but they ate little. They understandably didn't want to tell any more of their torture, and we didn't press them, knowing how helpless we were to bring charges against an occupying enemy. Their experience made me realize that in spite of my age I as a woman was vulnerable, too.

We hardly knew they were with us. I dusted and swept the floors, prepared meals with the last of the food Ivan had brought, and tried to keep busy with menial tasks that might keep me from thinking about our guests. Peelings that couldn't be eaten made their way to my compost pile, which seemed little higher than an anthill because nowadays I used nearly every edible scrap. Paul loved liver dumplings in soup, but now he got a simple turnip or potato soup with no meat broth. When thoughts of planting a spring vegetable garden sprouted in my imagination, I quickly weeded them out. It was impossible to plan even a day ahead.

The newspaper had been closed down, and in my own way I was glad. I didn't want to know any more than I already knew. Was I reverting to that simple girl who first went to work in Paul's lab?

In spite of several more attempts, Paul was unable to find the father; but the girls were convinced that they would have success when they insisted upon leaving after three days. We tried to dissuade them, but at the same time, I didn't have surplus food to share.

21 FEBRUARY | WEDNESDAY

Many years later I heard of young women frightened at the approach of Russian soldiers. Rather than being raped over and over and then left to die, they chose to cut their wrists and slowly bleed to death.

Our self-delusions had migrated with the birds several months ago. No songs came from bare branches. We were prisoners in our own home. If we fled now, we would be judged Nazis and probably shot.

A problem arose: who should go into town, an unavoidable trip even though little food was available. If I went, I could be raped. If Paul went, he could be conscripted. Many sent their elders or their children on errands and prayed for their safe return. Fritzi was too young. The girls were gone; we worried about their safety and hoped they were with their father, somewhere in hiding, perhaps in the bordering woods.

Many years ago vast areas were planted with trees, laid out in grids, numbered, and tended by government officers as a crop. Large ones were cut for lumber; young ones replaced them. The same grids still exist at the borders of the forests near towns, but industrialization and changing times left the interiors dense and untended. Seeds begat younger trees, bushes filled in, and eventually a nearly impenetrable wilderness took over, which even we natives didn't enter.

Another town boundary is the river Anklar, to the north. Most bridges across it won't support heavy motorized vehicles like tanks and loaded trucks. It is not navigable and serves only as a source of water when needed and as a place for children to frolic in hot weather. Spreading away from town to the south and east are meadows and fields, cultivated for crops just as they have been since medieval times when agriculture was carried on outside a village and farmers returned to the fortified center after a day's labor.

All of us townspeople knew well the paths of the western woods. We took refuge there from the summer's heat, meandering through the shading pines. Beyond the footpaths the thicket of brambles and tall trees is so dense that the blue heavens can't be seen. Many evacuees escaped in that direction, perhaps not knowing the futility.

"Paul, I hear noises in the flat next door."

I woke and roused my husband. The grilled gate to our common cellar clanged shut. Even though our bedroom was upstairs, the sound of the heavy metal gate's closure resounded through the old brick building.

"Hurry! Hannah. go hide! I shall go to the cellar to see what is going on."

I dashed downstairs, into the kitchen, and up into the loft. Soon there were voices and steps coming up from the cellar. Peeking down through a slit in the floor, I could see three soldiers and hear them speaking Russian. Their metal belt buckles and helmets clattered on the kitchen table. Evidently they were planning to stay a while.

"Where weapons? More lights."

It was the middle of the night.

"We have no weapons. We are a peaceful family."

"Liar! All Germans lie."

They were opening cupboards, throwing drawers on the floor. They cursed and kept shouting "Liar, liar."

Their vocabularies seemed limited to swearing and demanding.

The ruckus woke Fritzi upstairs, so he sleepily went down to the kitchen. Naturally the soldiers frightened him, and he whimpered quietly. I thanked the Lord that he didn't ask where Mutti was while Paul tried to comfort him. I cringed as I watched them quickly fill two suitcases. I couldn't tell what they were taking, but we didn't have much of value except for Paul's scientific equipment. My "equipment" consisted of frying pans, a soup pot, rather ordinary dishes, brooms, dustpans, and some good cleaning rags that I was constantly misplacing. The Russians couldn't take away my treasured compost pile. I had one recipe book I seldom used. I didn't need it for Paul's favorites. What could they be taking? I feared calling out or protesting. My husband was helpless. I think they partially believed Paul, that we had nothing, but they still stuffed their cases.

We knew that soldiers had gone rampant while plundering the empty houses because they believed that everyone who had lived in them and who had fled had to be Nazis. But not us! They had no reason to punish us, or to rob us.

"Vas dort?" one asked, pointing to the loft. None of the Russians had ever searched up there before. My heart was in my throat. I thought of the girls. How lucky that they were no longer hiding with us. I prayed for Paul's life should he try to protect me. What would become of Fritzi if they carried me off? Should I resist if they found me? Could I?

I crouched in a corner, covered with some rags, knowing I would be found because the soldiers were so thorough.

"Good Lord, help me!" I prayed. Soon I could see two heads rising on the ladder, their pistols pointed. Paul followed them and came over to where I hid, pulling off the rags to reveal me before the soldiers could kick the pile with their heavy boots. Valiantly he took me by the arms and pulled me up. Angry curses in Russian.

"Schnell! Schnell!" They pushed us toward the ladder, and forced us down.

Fritzi ran to Paul. One commanded, "Go search pillows, beds. Germans liars mit guns in beds."

He tore the coverlet from the sofa we had moved to the kitchen and threw it on the floor. Two soldiers went upstairs while we three sat immobile as statues, guarded by the third soldier, who fingered a gun on the table. We heard them tramping in the bedrooms and again the sound of bureau drawers being thrown onto the floor. They came down carrying nothing, for they had already filled their cases. Fortunately, that day they were more interested in plunder than pleasure so they picked up their heavy metal helmets and belts from the table, grabbed the suitcases, and left.

I was too exhausted both mentally and physically to start the cleanup. My mother had taught me to keep a house impeccable, but I truly didn't care any more.

Why hadn't we left Liegenbruch when we had the chance? Fleeing with Fritzi would have been less dangerous than remaining behind for such indignities, such barbarity.

"We must try to get some sleep," suggested Paul. "It is not yet light, and if sleep does not come, at least rest."

Fritzi went into his bedroom and cried out in dismay, "Look what they've done!"

We found feathers over the two beds, over the floor, over everything. They had cut the pillows and mattresses to pull out all the stuffing. I suppose they were looking for a weapon. Besides cleaning up this mess, I still had the kitchen to put back in order and drawers to pick up. You'd think they could have squeezed the pillows to feel if a hard gun was inside. We told Fritzi to come in with us for the rest of the night.

In our bedroom they had not overlooked our pillows and mattress either. Partially broken bureau drawers lay spilled on the floor. I was glad they hadn't bothered with my clothes in the closet. Simple dresses, neatly pressed, not worth taking. Of course, we got no more sleep that night.

I was living my nightmare, thankful that I had been spared so far, but not others. Each night piercing cries came from adjacent streets as poor women and girls were hauled off for assault. I knew it mattered little that I was neither young nor pretty. Years later I heard that the brutes had mutilated girls' private parts and cut swastikas into their breasts. What motivated such barbarity? Had they lost brothers in the fighting, sisters to rapists in Stalingrad, parents to mortar shells? How much revenge did they want?

22 FEBRUARY | THURSDAY

When daylight arrived, I went out alone for a short while, but not too far. I simply had to get away from the rubble in my own house. It would have been nice to take Fritzi with me to the pond. We used to enjoy our walks, finding peaceful relaxation feeding the ducks, but now I didn't want him to see the devastation nearby. The pond was frozen over anyway. No carefree townspeople were skating there. No local band played an afternoon concert. Summer was long gone and with it our former life.

Late winter winds were especially piercing that year, and the January snow was deep. I'd never welcomed the cold months, but what choice did I have? Oh, yes, I'd read in my geographies about places where the sun always shines and where warm breezes kiss the land. I wanted to experience a hot wind blowing from the desert, but those winds belonged in books on the shelf next to the fairy tales of Grimm. The temperature was near freezing, and I wished for a heavy February snow to cover the debris in the yards and streets: broken furniture, muddy linens, children's toys, wagons, wooden boxes, clothing for youngsters and women. Whatever the troops didn't have a use for was viciously discarded.

I returned home quite soon, lamenting all the wastes of war. After viewing the trash outside, I found cleaning up the feathers didn't seem such an onerous task. I made a new pillow casing from another pillowcase. Old quilts padded Paul's and my slashed mattress, and a clean sheet on the bed gave some sense of order. Again, thanks be to the Lord that the Russians didn't want our linens. Paul offered to help me, but I urged him to get some fresh air as I had.

"At last the Russian are starting to cart off the corpses," he reported upon his return. "Because I had not walked far from the flat since the street battles, I was unaware of the horrifying specter in town."

"I hope they don't want you to help again. I'll never forget your state of mind after burying the refugees."

"This morning I kept my distance. As you know, thousands of wagons and trucks and tanks have passed through the streets, headed for Berlin. They all simply rolled over the bodies in their way."

Quite soon came the dreaded knock on the door. They wanted Paul. I feared for his life in the hands of those brutes when he wasn't home by noon; Fritzi and I ate potatoes and cabbage. The pickles were gone; the blue enamel milk pitcher sat empty. I had some brown bread for Paul, but he hadn't returned by dark.

Missing his father, Fritzi was infected with my apprehension. I hated to keep him inside every day. Paul spoke of the other family on the block. Their son was about Fritzi's age, in the same school, but I didn't want to visit them in search of a "play date." Resigned, I put him on our bed after supper and read him some of Heine's poems. Even if he didn't understand all the words, he loved the rhyme and rhythm. At last he fell asleep, and as I lay praying through the ceiling to some god I hoped was listening, I heard Paul at the door. I ran downstairs.

"Come, come, let's go into the kitchen. I have some food waiting for you."

"Food, Hannah? I cannot think of eating. You will not believe what I have been forced to do, but then again, you will believe me."

"Let's go sit down in the kitchen."

Paul sat a long time in silence. At first he cradled his head in his arms on the table. Then came his running his fingers through his thick hair, creating furrows as if to let the air make its way to his brain. Straightening his back, staring in front of him, he related in a zombie's monotone: "The Russian soldiers forced me to go into houses to find bodies. They accompanied me with their pistols in hand. They also had another fellow, Römpagel, in tow."

I interrupted, hoping to break his trance: "I had no idea that there would be bodies inside houses. The thought never occurred to me."

"Oh, yes, indeed. They were there. I found the charred bodies of people who died in the fires. Other corpses that were not burned were probably of fleeing refugees who sought shelter. Some must have been exhausted from running and chose suicide out of despair. Hannah, I shall spare you the details. I shall just say that quite a few bodies were in advanced decomposition."

"Ach, what horror! But you're at home now. You must take care of yourself. At least sip a little broth."

"Those Russians expected me, as a resident, to identify the bodies. How could I recognize a pile of rotting flesh? I nearly fainted from the stench. Townspeople? Refugees? I didn't know."

"You haven't eaten since breakfast. Please sip some broth."

"That's not the end of it, Hannah. We also had to go to the road leading west out of town. They wanted us to identify the bodies of people who had been run over. Those poor souls could hardly be distinguished as human beings, flattened like flies hit with a swatter. But to recognize who they were--impossible! I hurried home as quickly as possible."

"So you could make no identifications anywhere?"

"No. Some were hanging from rafters in the houses. Others lay on the floor, wrists slashed and rotting in stagnant pools of dried blood, knives still in their hands. I suppose some had shot themselves or taken poison. In the condition we found them, how could we know? We were no forensic experts. Römpagel and I worked together. I never knew him before, but his situation is similar to ours and his repulsion equaled mine."

Anguish was tearing his soul.

"Oh, Paul, what has happened to our safe little world?"

"We have to answer that question honestly. We can imagine how our troops might have behaved abroad. Common foot soldiers are all alike in wartime, no matter what their country. Some of these Russians experienced pillaging of their villages, rape of their women, burning of their homes, random shootings of the innocent. They've been storing up hatred for us. Now we are experiencing the eruption."

"I know you're right."

"If only I had taken you away earlier, spared you and our son. I flog myself daily for my blind trust."

"No, no Paul. You've always been an honorable man, rational, a good husband and father. But our world now is no longer governed by honor and goodness."

"All logic and humanism are gone. Total chaos."

"At least we have some order here in our home, in spite of the looters."

"Yes, they have left us with some dignity, some sort of normal daily living."

We sat silent. Each of us with private thoughts.

Then he continued: "In places the demolished furnishings and linens were piled a foot high. The stench was beyond description. I waded through broken porcelain, clothing, spilled food, feathers from featherbeds. We actually had to dig through the filth for abandoned bodies because the Russians simply threw mats or rugs over them or shoved them aside."

"Oh, Paul," I whimpered. "How dreadful! Such horror! If only the Russians would leave soon and let us find some peace again. There's nothing more for them in our town."

I myself felt ravaged and was unconsciously pulling at my hair with both hands. Paul stood up and took me into his trembling arms. We stood, immobile, finding our entire situation beyond verbal expression. I persuaded him to go upstairs with me to bed.

Hours are longest when one lies awake listening to the pounding of artillery--at first far off, then close by, then again in the distance. I found a peculiar comfort in the loud noises, knowing they were far away. It was the fainter noises that tensed my back. Had looters returned? How did they get in?

I thought about our first conversations with the friendly officers. They commented on how rich we were, how rich our farmers were. Extra pots and pans. Plates and cups for more than we three. Indoor plumbing. Closets filled with more garments than we could wear at one time. Pictures on the walls. Books on the shelves. By their standards we were rich. And what did they want? Liquor and watches.

23 FEBRUARY – 7 MARCH

In spite of the occupation and the mass exodus of fellow townsmen, we stayed on in Liegenbruck. I couldn't bear the thought of leaving on foot in the cold late-February winter with a young child who was not especially strong. Of course, Paul didn't suggest departure either. We weren't eating as we used to, but we got by.

Each year I had been storing, as my mother had, canned produce and preserved meats, foods that we had steadily been consuming. My treasured, weathered wooden barrel was of a size to hold about ten pounds of sugar for preserving fruits and making jams. Now it was nearly empty. Even our stash of potatoes from my garden had to be rationed. Getting soap was out of the question. Gone was the open market for fresh produce. Fritzi missed butter on his bread; we substituted lard until all meats and fats were unavailable. Much that I had saved was taken by Russian soldiers when they searched the cellar for schnapps and wine; and what they didn't steal they threw onto the floor, where it lay, rotting amidst broken glass. I had no inclination to clean up the mess. My former pride in keeping a clean and orderly house had been destroyed.

Paul had a big appetite. Eating three or four eggs when they were available and at least seven to nine potatoes at a meal was nothing unusual. Our potatoes, grown in rich northern European soil, are yellow. Their distinctive flavor is beyond description. A friend told me that in the U.S. a person finds it difficult to stop eating popcorn. Here it is potatoes.

Paul went to the door one morning, dreading he would be called for another identification ordeal, but Russians were bringing soap and dirty clothes for us to wash. They said they would be coming every day.

"Oh, Hannah. They will certainly pay us for our work, some food or perhaps some milk for Fritzi, if we ask."

Ja, ja, they promised. Both Paul and I scrubbed mud-caked uniforms, socks stiff with stale sweat, shirts reeking with perspiration odor. We never knew when dirty clothing would be delivered, though we preferred mornings so that they might dry outside on the line. In the chilling February air damp garments often froze stiff. Then we had to bring them inside and drape them over the furniture from late afternoon until morning, when the soldiers returned to bring us more. Sometimes I used their soap to wash our own garments. If ours were not dry before the Russians returned, I tucked them away at bedtime, out of sight in the loft, and brought them out again after the soldiers left.

When several days had passed and we had received no pay for our labors nor milk for Fritzi, Paul asked again for some compensation.

Ja, ja they told us again, but those were just more empty promises. We got nothing.

Paul's initial pleasure at our menial, unpaid employment turned more sour than unripe cherries. As the war progressed, I became accustomed to his vacillations. He was a tortured man. At the university, he was in charge of his classes and research. Students and colleagues respected him. Now he was in charge of washing the enemies' clothes and reduced to being a man around the house, where I had been in charge. Although washing clothing was professionally degrading, he felt some pride in thinking he might have found a way to provide income and food for his family. A failed plan.

He continued questioning his decision to remain in Liegenbruck rather than to have fled eight years earlier, but back then it seemed the wise course. He loved being a father to Fritzi, while lamenting the affairs of the world into which we had brought our child. Prolonged periods of pessimism tore at him. When he grasped slight glimmers of hope, such as compensation for the laundry, I didn't know if he truly was emerging from his gloom or if he was simply trying to cheer me. We shared our concerns, but there was a part of him to which the door always was closed.

About the same time, an official of the security police, certainly not more than 22 or 23 years old, began his daily harassing. He called himself something that sounded like Major Sytzko. When he first came, Paul invited him inside and took him into the living room.

The officer indicated I should follow. His pink face was very like that of a pig: large nostrils rather in front of instead of below a flat nose. His neck was very short, almost swallowed up in the collar of his uniform, of which he was obviously very proud. When he took off his hat, indicating that he would stay, I noticed his coal-black hair was slicked down with pomade and in sharp contrast with the coloring of his face. Because he suspected Paul of being a Nazi, his interrogations were clever, sinister, cunning, in spite of his limited German vocabulary.

"You, Nazi. I see pictures family! Show me books! Show me medals."

Of course, there were no pictures of Paul with Party insignia or with Party officers. Scientific texts and classical literature provided no fodder for his appetite. He would find no signs of party affiliation amongst my favorite poets, all sitting next to each other on the shelf: Goethe, Schiller, Uhland, Eichendorff, Hebbel, Keller, Heine. When Paul nodded to me, I carefully took some of the beloved volumes from my bookcase. How dare he put his loathsome hands on my treasures. The official quickly glanced at them before pushing them aside. He then asked again for pictures and medals.

An engraving of Dresden from a point on the Danube was also hanging on the wall. Paul had bought it at a dear price many years before I knew him. It was by a famous artist, and I knew he was relieved that the officer ignored it. But he did spot evidence of guilt when he pointed to the picture of Nietzsche.

"Dort, on wall. Guardian angel Third Reich."

He was almost manic in his fiendish glee.

"I have owned that picture of Nietzsche for twenty years. He was no advocate of National Socialism. The ignorant Nazis chose only certain words of his, words which suited them, which supported their causes."

As Paul spoke, he lifted his eyebrows. His language, as usual, was academic, somewhat stiff. He held his hands flat on his thighs, spreading his fingers for emphasis. I don't know how much the official really could understand or how he would interpret the gestures, though his comprehension was probably better than his ability to express himself in our language. He may have been using the only German phrases that he had memorized, but we knew that Russian officers could be devious, and this one might have been trying to catch us off guard by pretending not to understand anything that Paul and I might say to each other. Each of his visits was a repeat of the previous one.

"You, Nazi. I see pictures family! Show me books! Show me medals."

We felt persecuted by those repetitious interrogations, but what could we do? He changed tactics at his last visit when he started searching through Paul's papers. Fortunately he found documents critical of the party and denouncing its atrocities. Though seemingly satisfied, his parting words were "I come back." The officers with whom we had previous experience had language skills and manners more polished.

"What relief, Hannah. At last we have convinced our conquerors that we are willing to wash their clothes, to bury the dead, to clear the debris, and best of all-- they know we are not Nazi spies. They trust us. For the first time I can feel hope."

His words of cheer did nothing to lift my spirits. I persuaded him to go to the commandant to learn if we had been cleared at last of being Nazis. He was reluctant, but went ahead only to find out that the major had not been under official orders to question us at all. He simply was entertaining himself and reporting to no one. We wondered if he had been reprimanded, for he didn't come back to torment us. I suppose that while the common soldiers were busy pillaging, the officers found their own diversions, like cats playing with mice.

In spite of our cooperation by taking in wash, our flat was not immune to invasion. I'll never forget that horrid day when six drunken soldiers broke in!

"What do you want?" questioned Paul.

The first soldier bristled.

"Give schnapps," another demanded, as they started opening cupboard doors and drawers.

"We have none," Paul told them. "You Russians have taken all of it away."

"Liar! Liar! Liar! You Germans all liars."

"We have none."

One soldier pointed his gun at Paul:

"Twenty minutes, one liter alcohol!"

It was impossible, but we knew those men were capable of anything.

"As I told you, we have no schnapps, but come with me to the cellar. Perhaps we can find something else that you want."

Paul walked to the door opening to the stairs down. I followed him to help.

Well, I knew they would find nothing but broken glass and rotting jam that we had not finished disposing of. With all the laundry to do each day, little time remained for cleaning up, even if I had the heart to do so.

"Liar. Liar. All Germans lie," they roared.

In their rage two of them pulled out German sabers, brandishing the blades in my husband's face. Both were direct descendants of Lucifer himself, substituting sabers for pitchforks.

"Please, please," I screamed. I pleaded. I got on my knees, praying that they spare us.

I succeeded only in enraging one of them further as his eyes shot hatred toward me. He hit Paul on the side of the head with his weapon. Encouraged, a second one slashed his cheek. The others looked on with laughs and smiles and encouraging Russian phrases whose words we didn't understand but whose intent we did.

The mounting anger of the two assailants increased at our hopeless state and at the sight of blood. Paul suffered two more blows to his face, then a puncture to his abdomen and a slashed leg.

I started up the stairs, planning to run into the street for whatever help I could find. No longer could I stay in the basement, watching Paul slowly being murdered. Two of the Russians noticed my movement and grabbed at me, pushing me down into the cellar again. Evidently sobered at the sight of so very much blood, all six suddenly fled.

13-17 MARCH
TUESDAY TO SATURDAY

Our apprehension increased each time we heard a knock on the door. Would it be the security official again? The drunken soldiers? I prayed not! Some officer, perhaps to investigate the previous day's violence? More laundry? We had no more idea of who was at the door than we did of how the war was progressing beyond the door. We knew only of our own ignorance.

Paul remained in bed for quite a few days, resting and regaining some strength. I had dressed and bandaged him to the best of my ability, limited as were our medications and my medical knowledge. My previous experience had been confined to cut fingers and scraped knees. Fortunately his wounds were mostly to his flesh and would heal in time. Both of us had suffered shock and found it onerous to keep up a semblance of normalcy for Fritzi. My nightmares had subsided, probably because the increased violence during the day so exhausted me that my body needed uninterrupted sleep.

I knew we were not the only ones suffering, but when I couldn't get out, didn't dare go out, I began to pity myself. Fortunately it was short-lived, for one day friendly faces appeared at the door, a family of three, strangers to us.

"Hello, we're the Grammen family and hope you can take us in."

I was taken aback. Of course, we had taken in Herr Hirsch and the two girls, but how could we provide for three more mouths? Paul was still upstairs in bed, so I couldn't consult with him at once or let him make the quick decision.

"Where are you coming from?"

They looked honest and desperate. I thought Paul would have been compassionate, but I needed to know more.

"Do come in and tell me about yourselves."

Frau Grammen was a small, slender woman, just a little over five feet tall. She wore her brown hair pulled into a bun on her neck and held in place with large yellow and brown celluloid pins. Wisps of naturally wavy hair escaped the pins and framed her face. In her hands she was nervously twisting a handkerchief while forcing a smile with quivering lips. Her kind hazel eyes responded gratefully to my invitation. With the couple was a young boy, Rolf, several years older than Fritzi. Rolf appeared healthy and wore a black leather cap. When he politely removed it, I could see his blond hair combed back in a stiff pompadour. In comparison with Fritzi, he had a lot more flesh on his bones and seemed untouched by circumstances.

Herr Grammen was taller than his wife, but both were considerably shorter than I was. He, like his wife and son, wore a heavy loden great coat, and a dark felt hat pushed down on his graying hair above a high forehead. Because his chin was clean-shaven, I assumed that he might have been in his own home that morning, as his wife stated. I riveted my attention to his lips beneath a thick mustache because he was visibly shaken and had trouble getting words out. His suit was well tailored, his shirt clean and starched, and a tie and vest attested to his possibly being in a profession or business.

"Russian soldiers came to our house this morning. When I opened the door, they pushed me aside and stalked through the house, looking in all the rooms. Then they said that they needed our house and that we must be out of it in 30 minutes."

"What a shock that must have been for you," I empathized.

"They said we could take with us some possessions and provisions. Our little cart is in the street."

I couldn't refuse.

"We're living on very little food and have really nothing to offer except a place to stay for a short while. I certainly commiserate with your plight."

"Oh, a place to rest is all we ask. We have nowhere to go."

"Then go bring your cart into the house."

Herr Grammen shook my hand in gratitude and said, "I'll go out for it. Come help me, Rolf."

A few minutes later, the two came running into our hallway.

"They're gone. All gone! Some soldiers took the cart."

Tears began to run down Frau Grammen's unblemished cheeks.

"The drunken animals even took our wedding rings from our fingers!" she lamented.

Though we had scarcely enough food for ourselves, I'm glad I didn't refuse the Grammens. They helped me move Fritzi with his single bed into our bedroom, and we set up a makeshift sleeping bag for Rolf with the last of our spare comforters and blankets next to the extra bed in Frizi's room. My mother and grandmother had made patchwork comforters and quilts from men's woolen suits, too worn to be of further use but still providing sections large enough for squares. Paul's mother never had to resort to such frugality, so he had nothing like them. He wanted to get out of bed to help, but I insisted he continue to rest from his trauma. He trusted my judgment in helping those people.

It seemed as if their presence helped to heal his wounds, for within another day he was out of bed. Our life fell back into a routine. It was almost like the old days of getting Paul and Fritzi off each morning. Frau Grammen helped me to clean the rotting debris from the cellar and to wash the Russians' clothes.

I was grateful for her help since Paul was no longer able to carry his load, and the amount of dirty clothes didn't dwindle. Frau Grammen's hands soon resembled mine, rough and swollen from handling wet garments in the cold wind. We enjoyed seeing Rolf and Fritzi read together, and Paul had a companion. On the next day at eight o'clock in the morning and on the following three mornings Herr Grammen had to appear before the Russian commandant to tell all he knew about the Nazis. He was conflicted.

"The Party members had hardly left town before the Russians arrived. On the one hand, I hate the Nazis; on the other hand, I didn't want to betray my fellow townsmen. What was I to do?"

"Could you give them names?" I asked. I didn't even know who was a member and who wasn't.

He evaded my question and said, "The Russians didn't believe in a full-scale flight of all the local members. They told me that seven days after their advance to Liegenbruch they were finding Nazis around."

Paul told him about his interrogation by the Russian major who suspected him of being a Nazi.

"I believe they are searching ant holes and termite canals in search of Nazis and think they are discovering some. After a while everything will turn out well. Believe me. The Russians will consider all the suffering they have caused here and leave."

I had to bite my tongue. "Why do you think they will leave?"

"Once they have confiscated all the belongings that party members left behind, what of value is left? They must know that guilty consciences and fear drove out the real enemies."

"With the town nearly empty," Herr Grammen continued, "of what use is questioning me every day?"

"Surely they're testing your loyalty, and they want to know about the rest of us who are here. About every single one of us."

"And once they know we're innocent, what then?"

Paul optimistically continued, smiling gently, "We shall make a treaty. You may be appointed the leader of a new administration to create order again."

I knew Paul was forcing himself to present a positive face. Herr Grammen painted the entire situation in the darkest tones and was exacerbating Paul's deepening depression. Perhaps with his lofty tone, he was seeking from Herr Grammen some of the respect of students and colleagues that was missing from his life. Perhaps he really was becoming more positive. He had a sense of hope that he was contributing in his own way to reorganization by taking in laundry. We were buying credit with the Russians.

For as much as we wanted to continue helping the Grammens, our house was very crowded at night with damp clothing everywhere. Frau Grammen worked tirelessly next to me while her husband was gone, but she was a frail woman and unused to such labor. I truly don't know what Herr Grammen decided to tell and to withhold.

After five days I was relieved when they decided they could leave without danger. I assumed they were heading west with the permission of the Russians, though they didn't confide in us. We never inquired about their lifestyle or what was Herr Grammen's occupation, and they didn't tell.

Fritzi spent most days inside the house, and we knew it was a boring life for a young boy to watch his parents wash clothing for hours at a time. He missed Rolf. His school had long been closed, and his friend Heinrich was gone, too. We locked the doors to our flat and spent quiet evenings engrossed in our readings or tutoring Fritzi. I was content that Paul had recovered and that our life had settled into a routine again, but who knew for how long?

21 MARCH | WEDNESDAY

Paul's wounds were almost completely healed, and with them his periods of depression. We believed that some of the Russians had moved on because the loads of dirty clothing had ceased arriving. The incident with the drunken soldiers was the last invasion of our home, and we started to become complacent and content, in spite of our deprivations.

Feeling remiss for confining Fritzi so much, we relented when he wanted to play with Rudi, a 12-year-old boy in the block and the only child left nearby. His experience with Rolf Grammen had whetted his appetite for companionship his own age. The two boys played back and forth in each other's yards, usually under our watchful eyes. From being out of doors in the fresh air, Fritzi seemed more healthy, with a slight glow to his cheeks.

One day when he was out playing, we heard an explosion. Was it the Russians starting to destroy what remained of the town before leaving? Paul and I suddenly rushed out to find Fritzi to bring him inside. Where was he? Not in our yard. In the street in front of Rudi's house we found the boys screaming with fright. We took their hands and hurried home. Hysterical and white as cheese, they eventually calmed down and we heard no more detonations. Fritzi explained: "Rudy found a funny round ball with a pin in it. We were going to play catch after he pulled the pin out."

"Oh, good Lord! A hand grenade!"

What a wonder the boys were still alive! We followed them to where they had been playing and saw that the nearby trees had suffered.

I asked, "Did you know what the ball was? That it was an explosive?"

Rudi replied, "We thought it was all right. My father saw us playing with it."

At that, Paul stiffened with fury. He didn't know the father, but had nodded to him from time to time as they passed each other on the street. He took Rudi with him when he went to confront the stupid bloat who opened the door.

"Rudi here was almost killed. Did you know that?"

The boy's father was a burly man about forty years old. He was wearing a dirty undershirt and open vest. After he removed his leather cap, Paul saw short-shorn brown stubby hair sprouts.

The father said nothing. His pock-marked face betrayed no emotion.

"Rudi tells me that you saw the boys playing with a grenade. You did nothing!"

"*Nein, nein.* You're wrong there. I told them it was dangerous."

"Why didn't you take it away from them?"

The man had the empty eyes of a cow that reflected the vacancy behind them.

"You can't blame me. I'm proud of myself for telling them, but they didn't pay any attention. I warned them."

Paul returned home, lost in the stupor of the man's logic, the idiot. He should have been blown up with the trees. We were sobered at the thought of having almost lost our beloved child. Paul then decided to go out to comb the area in search of more explosives. And he found many! When the next Russian sentry came by, the grenades were on display in our back yard, where we could guard them, even though we could be certain the boys would not approach them. Paul took the sentry to see his collection, hoping that he would make arrangements to have them taken away and confiscated. We couldn't have foreseen his reaction.

"Say, that's quite a collection," he laughed, shrugging his shoulders and walking away.

He must have reported the cache or the explosion to some higher official because the next day a Russian controller searched our neighbor's house. There he found cartridges, which Rudi's father claimed were "souvenirs." There he also uncovered pieces of SS uniforms. Before that family could be charged with responsibility for any of the evidence found, the Russian officer mysteriously disappeared. We learned this fact when soldiers came to search our house again.

This time they found soiled tablecloths and sheets in the loft where I had hidden myself earlier. These were the linens Paul had collected from the street to save for our neighbors who had fled. So busy with the laundry of the Russians, we hadn't had time to clean the salvaged items.

The searchers were convinced that those sheets and towels had been soiled in a fight with the missing officer and hidden to conceal evidence. They took out their guns, and their accusations of murder would have resulted in an actual murder in our flat had not an officer abruptly appeared. Saved at the last moment! No day was without harrowing trials or freedom from tension. I doubt Paul had ever known fear and loathing before. He tried to temper it with thoughts of the Nazi atrocities.

28 MARCH | WEDNESDAY

"Good frau. You must meal for us cook."

At the door stood seven Russian soldiers. Their arms were loaded with bags of various sizes, and they pushed their way in as if they lived in our house. We had never seen any of them before, but we were easy to find. Few German houses were still occupied. White flags distinguished flats like ours, where inhabitants remained.

I turned and went down the hall to the kitchen. We had been accustomed to Paul's being conscripted for labor, but this was the very first time that my personal labor was demanded. My husband had always kept me in the shadows, or up in the bedroom with Fritzi, or in the back yard bending over plants-- anywhere but where the soldiers would notice me. We supposed they had gone from white flag to white flag until they found a woman at home.

At once they unloaded chickens, potatoes, beans, a veal roast, cabbage, cauliflower, and so much more. Obviously they had no conception of how long it would take to cook those foods. The veal roast would require several hours. I put it into a roasting pan with some onions and potatoes. But first I had to scrub and peel the potatoes. And the chickens were not ready. Their heads had to be chopped off, their feathers plucked, their bodies singed, their feet removed.

Could I put those feet aside as if they were scrap, saving them for a broth another day? Should I roast or boil the birds? Frying as an alternative was eliminated because they brought no lard. I should have rejoiced at the bounty before me, but the task seemed overwhelming. How I longed for a kitchen helper, but it would have been unthinkable to ask them to assist, nor did I feel I could ask Paul.

He chatted with them. His Russian was limited as was their German, but a hand on the chest with the word *Heimat* told that they missed their homes. The same for families and *Haus*. Some were more fluent than others and translated for each other. We hadn't chairs for so many, but they didn't seem to mind sitting on the floor. These were not the coarse and mean soldiers we had recently encountered but very young men, actually boys. Were they reserves following the more experienced army? While they waited, they asked for schnapps and cigarettes. Of course, we had none. Some of my fatigue disappeared as I watched them play with Fritzi. There was so little laughter and joy in his life nowadays, but here he was smiling and snickering.

I suppose the scent of food cooking nearby soothed the tensions of everyone. And what pleasure I had placing the feast before the soldiers and having our family share it, even though the preparation had taken at least three hours.

This group adopted us as parents or friends and started stopping by to chat, two or three at a time. Then they prolonged their visits by staying several hours. Most had had few experiences with domestic chores. They watched me wash and rinse our family's clothing, amazed at a double rinsing. I had put aside some soap each time the Russians came for us to do their laundry, so we could frugally ration it to ourselves. Seeing me boiling potatoes was a new experience for them. Did they never go into their mothers' kitchens?

When they brought coffee or tea, they were surprised how quickly the beverage could be prepared. I guess they thought the same was true of all foods until they saw how many hours I had spent on the first feast. I was able to make them understand when they wanted future meals they should bring a larger quantity of just one kind of meat so that I could more quickly have the meal ready. Such camaraderie was welcome, and we knew they would never accuse us of lying.

Unfortunately for all of us, they had to move on toward Berlin. Naively we expected similar good will from their replacements, but that was not the case. New troops were always coming through town, excited by the prospect of plunder. The ransacked flats offered nothing.

A month had passed since the occupation was complete. No civil administration had been established. No order prevailed. We were like stalks of corn left in the field after harvest, worthless, waiting to be mowed down.

And the mower came to our house in the form of a wild crowd. Finding little of value to take, they vented their frustration in senseless destruction: Paul's scientific apparati, his typewriter, his camera. They might even have directed their anger on our persons had Fritzi not gone to our rescue by screaming through the street: "They want to kill my father. Come help us!"

Since Russians are almost universally fond of children, some officers paid attention to the little one's pleas and came to the flat. They drove out their countrymen and even took away part of the loot to return it to us. Our home was in shambles. At least I would not feel pressed to do spring cleaning. Damage was in the thousands of marks. But we were alive.

Protest was unthinkable. The officers usually stood up for their men and defensively kept referring to the German devastation in their own country to justify their conduct in ours. We could easily understand, but we were not Nazis. Why was our way of life being daily eroded through no guilt of our own? We had condemned Hitler and his henchmen and the whole heinous war. Paul grieved to see all the means of his professional life and his tools for providing for his family in the future being obliterated.

Either we or soldiers had removed so much food from our cellar that we were forced to live on a diet of potatoes three times a day. Even boiled potatoes, a food we usually enjoyed, became endlessly tedious. No fried potatoes because no lard. No flavorful potatoes cooked in bacon fat because no meat. Not even a speck of butter to put on the boiled potatoes.

Even though Paul's outer wounds had healed, he was seriously stressed deep inside. Still he remained kind and loving in his quiet way to Fritzi and to me. He could no longer go to the closed university. Forced to spend his time without his equipment, his papers and books gave little solace. And what comfort could he find in his own house, in a house rent asunder? And his professional identity? Also kaputt. But he calmed my anxiety, speaking with assurance that all would change. I appreciated his bravura.

I always prided myself on my housekeeping, perhaps being compulsive, but that was how I was trained by my mother. Now looking at empty shelves, books torn and lying topsy-turvey on the floors of every room, clothing scattered wherever it had been thrown, I had little inclination to establish order again, but for Fritzi's sake, I tried.

"It's so hard to keep things neat," I often complained. Now, with fewer belongings the task was easier. Knowing how hard I tried, Paul would give me his half smile of approval, the same smile I had loved so long ago when I was his student and when I worked for him in his lab.

One day, despondent, Paul wandered through the nearby streets. I worried that he might be picked up, but home confinement gnawed on his nerves.

"Hannah, Hannah," he called to me, returning from his short walk. "Just see what I have!"

It was a dead chicken he found in a yard nearby. I drew back at the reeking stench of the hen, now dead for several days. Still, I scrubbed and washed and washed and scrubbed till every trace of the foul odor seemed gone. Cleansing the chicken was a sacrifice of a considerable amount of water that we had saved in the bathtub. We had been without water for almost three weeks, and nearing the end of March our supply was nearly depleted, being used only for cooking and drinking. But oh! it would be worth stinting even more to eat meat. That bird came to life again in a sumptuous stew, flavored with an onion still in the ground in our garden. I can almost smell again the fragrance that overcame all my dismay at our tiny recent meals. And I was grateful to have a cooking pot. What a joyous festive meal that was! I shall never forget the pleasure on the faces of my loved ones as they savored the plates I set before them. Fritzi forked tender pieces of meat from the fat broth. The potatoes were saturated with flavor. I insisted that we eat very slowly to make each mouthful last as long as possible. No gourmet cook in a five-star restaurant could feel greater joy in pleasing the palates of patrons.

All of our daily life took place within the few hours of daylight because power for light fixtures was sporadic. We were grateful that the days were becoming somewhat longer, preserving our few remaining   candles. But we maintained some semblance of routine within the bounds of deprivation, anxiety, eternal harassment, and plundering.

In the dark evenings we taught Fritzi songs that we three sang together. I, of course, way off key, but what did that matter? Paul and I pulled out of the past fairy tales that we had enjoyed as children. Making up our own tales was perhaps the most fun. I awoke each day with amazement at being alive, but with trepidation I asked the ultimate question: "What were we waiting for?"

Those of us left in the town had little communication with one another. We feared the wrath of the Russians, who still suspected us of being Nazi plotters. We were eager for news of the front, but there were no reliable reports. Wild were the rumors. Firm were the convictions with which they were believed. Certain were the suspicions that all were lies.

We were aware that our German troops were still close, only some 12 kilometers from the city. Occasionally a German plane flew overhead. We didn't care. All we wanted was to know when the war would finally end.

"Oh, Hannah! Now we can get some news." Paul hurried to the trash pile, where he had stowed a radio for safekeeping.

"Fritzi, keep watch with your mother. Guard the doors and watch out the windows in case the Russians pay a surprise visit."

"We knew the danger involved as he brought the coveted English radio into the house and plugged it into the wall. The German penalty for listening to broadcasts from outside the country was three and a half to five years imprisonment. He felt that the risk was less now with Russians in charge, but the old fear remained. We craved release from limbo. The Yanks had crossed the Rhine at Remagen and at several other places. Paul dared not listen for long before cautiously replacing it with the refuse, keeping it in position for listening the next day. Our happiness when we went to bed was so great that we could hardly sleep. How strange, though, to be caught in the middle between our "enemy's" victories and our own country's approaching defeat.

29 MARCH | THURSDAY MORNING

After a sleepless night we were jolted awake, like being attacked on two fronts. Simultaneously the front door and the yard door were broken in. A cold sweat of fright immediately drenched me. They were coming for Paul. The Russians had been grabbing men and women off the streets. No one ever heard of them again. What had they done? Where had they been taken? No one knew, but we did know that during those first days of occupation the entire male population from ages 17 to 50 was seized and carried off for hard labor without respect for circumstances. Women's sufferings were intense as they were separated from husbands and grown sons. Now I would be bereft and join them.

But I was wrong. Three Russians stormed in.

"You must leave. Five minutes!"

We were stunned speechless. Then Paul sputtered, "But what have we done?"

"We empty town. All out."

Panic overcame us. We couldn't think. After Paul's beating, the plundering, the intimidation, we thought we had endured all humanly possible. But to be forced to leave our home! And in five minutes!

My nerves were shredded, pulled first by one fear in one direction, then by another fear in the opposite direction. I didn't know whether to scream in agony or to fall to the floor in complete paralysis of will. We knew we couldn't fight them. Arguing was futile. The refugees that recently stayed with us a few days were like birds temporarily perching on a branch before flying off again. Would we also be refugees?

Five minutes! Good heavens! I started gathering whatever I thought we would need: good cutting knife, table ware, four or five plates, pots and pans, some matches, whatever staples I could readily stuff into my shopping bag. I could pack more than many other women could into a bag twice its size.

"I'll go to some of the abandoned houses to find a cart or wagon," Paul declared.

When he had a task to complete, Paul became absolutely absorbed and could shut out all around him, so I trusted he would find a cart and gather many essentials in the shortest time. We had no time to confer by asking, "Do you have this? Did you pack that?"

I went upstairs to wake Fritzi and tell him to dress at once, thankful that I didn't have to quell his anxiety to answer questions. He seemed to intuit I had no time to be a nurturing mother. I wondered if he thought this was a birthday surprise. Meanwhile the Russians sat at the kitchen table, smiling and chatting among themselves. How I cringed to hear them laughing and shouting from time to time, *"Schnell, schnell."* I was nervous enough trying to think under such intense pressure.

In no time I made a modest pile of belongings near the door and loaded them into the small wagon Paul had found. Under duress how does one know what are the necessities to take along? April weather was always unpredictable. How long would we be gone? What was vital to take? Sturdy shoes to wear, long cotton stockings, woolen scarves, head kerchief, caps, a skirt, two short-sleeve shirts and changes of underwear for each of us, two extra trousers for Paul and Fritzi, sox . . . was that all?

There was no space for my treasured books or fragile phonograph records. Paul's scientific books that he kept at home were space-eaters and too heavy. We hadn't yet made a photo album, but I gathered a few pictures without sorting them. Into each article of clothing, I tucked a treasured keepsake to remind us some day in the future of who we are and were.

By that time the Russians stood outside the door, exhorting us to hurry, "*Schnell, schnell*." I had hastily grabbed some of Fritzi's clothes while waking him and insisted he put on his warmest boots and jacket and pants and sweater. He quickly dressed as instructed, and we were ready and outside within half an hour.

"Oh, Paul. The cruelest blow--to leave our home. At least it provided some safety and security up to now. This is the end."

He didn't reply. He was wearing his usual suit, but in the turmoil he'd been so distraught that he left without a hat or his leather jacket. He did wear a heavy coat that I had "altered." It was a clear day in late March when we ordinarily wouldn't wear such heavy clothing, but it was easier to wear than to pack. Under my coat and sweater I was wearing an old plaid blouse that Fritzi liked. Years ago he had said it was full of teeter-totters. I hoped that we wouldn't be going far.

I don't use the word "alter" with the common meaning of making fit. After the first looting by the Russians I started my sewing "project."

Fritzi was intrigued to watch me cut squares from a sturdy dish towel and sew hidden pockets into our clothing. First I extended a pocket in Paul's trousers to make a deep hiding place just above his knee. When he had secured savings that we might not need immediately, I sewed shut the little compartment, creating a false bottom. Also the top of a pair of his underpants contained a flapped area that fitted into the small of his back. Inside the hem of my heaviest skirt lay another small sack. Paul's suit jacket contained an extra layer for flat items between the pocket and the lining, undetected if someone searched pockets. At the time I began my "project," I had no idea how often we'd subsequently be robbed. As soon as I finished making a hiding place, as if it were a small safe we stowed away some valuables in it. My only fear was that the soldiers would steal our clothing.

The Russians directed us through the streets to the main road leading west. On our way, we walked past bent bicycles, appropriated by the Russians and then destroyed after one use. We saw shattered shutters and doors. Electric wires lay exposed, protruding from windows and tangled in yards along with every conceivable kind of filth and debris.

On the road we joined a disconsolate band, as Paul and I took turns pulling the wagon. We were a long train of weary figures trundling at dawn. A shocking picture of neglected humanity. Almost no one had the strength to speak. I didn't ask Paul what he had packed. He didn't ask me.

At least one out of every five houses had been ravaged by fire or was smoldering as we passed by. Would they soon be torching ours? Urging us on, Russian troops constantly shouted *"Schnell! Schnell!"* Fritzi's arms were loaded with items we thought would not overtax his strength, and on his back was a small rucksack with his clothing. I frequently looked at him, watched him tilt his head back to dislodge from his forehead a golden lock.

Liegenbruch once was a city of over 100,000 residents. We knew many had fled besides Party members, but surprisingly 15,000 of us came crawling out of flats and houses. Some people in similar circumstances might have panicked like a small flock of birds startled as they rest on a sandbar during a southward flight. But we were not birds. We were Germans who evacuated in an orderly way. We supposed the reason for shoving us out was to provide the Russians an empty town for pillaging. How could their consciences later trouble them for stealing from vacant houses?

The sun rose higher in the morning sky when our herd left town. As the temperature increased, Fritzi began to complain about being too hot to keep on all the clothes he was wearing. Given the alternative of carrying them, he stoically smiled and said he'd be OK. The unpaved road leading west was full of puddles made by the last of the melting snow. Such a day was a rarity after the recent weeks of chilly winds. Ordinarily I'd be taking Fritzi to the nearby stream where he liked to sail his little green boat on a long string. Now we simply followed the crowd, creating our own stream.

Armed Russian soldiers walked along each side of our orderly column, urging the weaker elders: "*Schnell*!"

Every kilo that each person carried slowed his or her pace. Backs bent by age, many slowly shuffled along, barely able to lift their feet from the ground. Even though we didn't know their circumstances at the time, I thought of the first refugees from the east. They had left on their own volition. They had no leader. Perhaps they had perished, lost in the woods or along the road. What they did have was hope. Even though they feared the Russian onslaught, radio announcements of victory elated them. At the first of the year rockets were flying into London. Herr Goebbels assured his people that the British would surrender. His voice boasted, "Victory will be ours!"

Just 8 km. away from Liegenbruch lay a small village of 800 people: our destination. Little did the enemy care that Hilgendorf was not equipped to receive us. As we approached, I became more and more apprehensive about our reception, but those were wasted worries. The village was empty, plundered. We didn't know where the inhabitants had gone with probably no more possessions than we had brought with us, but nothing had been left behind. It was a poor village, so the Russians probably found few valuables to steal, but the slightest remnants were not to be found. Even the marshy soil offered nothing. Everyone immediately searched abandoned gardens for potatoes and carrots--anything for nourishment.

The Russians left us on our own to search for whatever living space we could find. Fifteen thousand people in a village for 800! Basic survival instincts emerged as we displaced vied for shelter. The Teutonic worship of order fell victim to more primitive behavior. Each room in each house had to accommodate five or six people.

"Hannah, you and Fritzi stay here by the river. I don't want to lose you in the crowding masses everywhere. I'll find shelter and come back for you."

"But what if you find a place and lose it while you are getting us?"

"Trust me. I'll have better luck alone."

What were we to do? We waited and waited. I envisioned my future home under a bush at the river. How could Paul alone reserve space for three in any room in any house? When he returned, he was smiling. "Come Hannah, Fritzi. I've found a good place for us."

29 MARCH | THURSDAY
MID-AFTERNOON

We followed him to a small shed with welcoming straw on the ground as a bed for the three of us. I noted there was no floor and the roof was caved in, but it was ours! We were alone and together, in a private abode, with no space for one single person more. The less we had, the less it took to satisfy us. Adjacent to the shed was a very small house, which reminded me of the teeny tiny houses in children's fairy tales. Nine of our fellow citizens took over its bedroom and parlor. Although tumbled down, it did have a stove. The squatters there had to tread lightly because the weak floor precariously gave way.

Settling in was no problem, and we were grateful the walk to Hilgendorf had been a short one. The toll was in psychic energy. Throughout our marriage we had trusted each other to make wise decisions. Neither of us had to remind the other of what had to be done or when. In some way our marriage was like a machine. Paul had his responsibilities; I had mine. We worked together to achieve a smooth operation, like cogs in a wheel, just as we had when I assisted him in his lab. I don't know if we knew each other well after all those years. Somewhere inside I had a secret corner where I swept thoughts that I didn't want to examine carefully. Perhaps even daydreams seeped in there to hide or grow. Was I content in my marriage? Or was discontent a luxury? How does one define happiness? We adored Fritzi. He was our joy, our daily delight. Dared I want more?

We were so entangled within the web the Russians had spun for us that we meekly acknowledged our helpless state with neither smiles nor tears. Paul used to be decisive. That day I admired his spirit in finding this shed on his own. Recently he had fluctuated from hope to despair. Sitting on the straw, he muttered with resignation: "Obviously we are going to perish, to die, if you like. We have no albumen. We have to find egg whites somewhere. Meat is out of the question. If only we could find a few grains of corn somewhere, anywhere."

I told him, "I have about three kilograms of flour that I grabbed at the last minute."

"And I picked up a carton of corn seed as I was packing."

Of course, it was nonsense to think that we would be in any one place long enough to plant and harvest corn, let alone protect our crop from hungry marauders. Yet we grasped the thinnest sliver of hope we could offer each other in our deepest despair so far. Never had we looked to the future with such sadness. Back home in Liegenbruch, we had become accustomed to deprivation. Sustenance had been minimal. Now the situation was catastrophic. We couldn't share with others the little we had carried away, nor could they do so with us. All along the riverbank were alders, birches, and shrubs for fuel, but ironically we had nothing to cook.

"Mommy, I'm so hungry. When are we going to eat?"

"Tomorrow, my son, we'll have more."

Fritzi's plaintive whimpers were to be played over and over like the leitmotif in a tragic opera, with slight variations in time and tone but always making me grieve. Would we have had a child had we known the consequences of remaining in Germany? His childhood had been snatched from him before he had much chance to be a happy boy. We hugged him and wished him Happy Birthday.

30 MARCH – 13 APRIL

Everything familiar was disappearing. Sorrow settled on us like dust, and it only increased during the following days.

"Oh, Paul. We'll starve here. How can we dare leave this little shed to get water?"

He had no answer and later said that he had turned away from me and left the hut to keep from bursting into sobs of grief as he looked at me and at Fritzi. He didn't know from hour to hour whether I might soon be snatched from him. I didn't know from hour to hour if he would be taken from me for hard labor or worse. Though he was over 50 years old, 58 in fact, he was tall and strong. He hadn't confided to me his plans, or rather the "ultimate plan," the "gift," until that day.

"Dear wife, I am prepared for the worst and have potassium cyanide ready for all three of us."

"Ach, mein Gott!"

"But I know I would never have the courage or cowardice to give that 'gift' to our little Fritzi. He is so woebegone, so pale, so trusting with his sunken little blue eyes."

I had to get away. I had nothing to say except "I'll go for some drinking water."

Water was constantly on our minds. Drinking water had to come from the neighboring farm, so I would be gone for some time. Time to digest Paul's revelation.

Several of our fellow evacuees in the village were hysterical at the lack of bread and water. More than one had skinny, wrinkled arms and a pinched face that showed deprivation. Paul hid in the wagon the three kilograms of flour I had packed; it was for Fritzi, who so badly needed protein for the growth of his frail little frame. I combed his blond hair several times a day and cut it short. We hadn't much soap with us, and water for washing had to be hauled from the brook. My brown skirt and brown sweater were heavy and serviceable, though becoming somewhat ragged and quite dirty. I was saving two cotton blouses for warmer weather and usually wore the plaid one.

We had no idea of how long we would be staying in semi-captivity. All thoughts of taking a family walk were out of the question. Someone had to stay in or near the shed at all times to guard the little we had. All three of us needed exercise, so Paul and I took turns walking around the village with Fritzi, but many more hours were vacant. Like a record player, I ran symphonies, sonatas, concerti through my brain, pretending that I was at a concert listening to the likes of Chopin or Mozart. Or I closed my eyes and returned to our parlor to look at my favorite books. And so I drifted with the spring breeze away from Hilgendorf.

Whatever the weather--and the days were becoming warmer--almost everyone spent waking hours out of doors, with the exception of our neighbors. Of the nine people in the next house, we usually had conversations with only three or four. The rest spent their days either inside or sitting on the remaining rail of a sagging fence, like a row of crows waiting to descend on a rotting carcass.

I often rested on the ground near the door of our hut to feel the sunshine warm my cheeks, trying not to think of the soft sunlight that came through the window of our parlor back in Liegenbruch. I wished for a pleasant spot to wash myself along the river, but privacy was impossible. Paul was the restless one and often took walks by himself while I guarded our possessions. Unable to wash my hair as frequently as needed, I'd been wearing a bandana like the farmers' wives wear in the fields. It gave me a sense of being more presentable, at least to myself. Often I gave Friti science lessons and told him the stories I knew from reading novels, or I described famous paintings and places, lamenting what a crime it was that the charismatic despot Hitler had the power to destroy our humanitarian heritage. As we sat in the sun, the tanks that rumbled by in the road made even the willow branches tremble.

Hilgendorf must have been a peaceful place to live at some past time. Now the abandoned houses crouched close together just like the displaced people inside them. All were sad, bedraggled, hopeless. How long would we be here? Would some occupation troops force us to stay, or would they permit us return to Liegenbruch?

Days piled upon days, all the same, just like the Russian doll boxes that contain exact copies of each doll in different sizes and repeat until depleted. Misery and the troops reigned over the village. The oldsters at the next house seldom left the premises. They knew that not far away an old man tried to protect an equally old woman from being raped and was severely beaten.

Fritzi was the only young child in our area of the village. Little by little his childhood disappeared. At first some of his classmates left. The first ones were Jews earlier in the war. Next fearful families in town packed up and fled. After the incident with Rudi and the grenade, he became completely reliant on Paul and me for companionship.

Without a doubt, all of the elderly next door were starved to the point of collapse. Greed spurred them to get food in any way they could. I feared to what depravity their hunger would drive them. They reviled poor Fritzi on all sides until he was completely intimidated by them. Usually the elderly enjoy having young children around, and Fritzi was very well behaved. Paul and I had been skimping on our daily rations in order to give our child more. Yet he couldn't fully comprehend when his clear, trusting eyes looked pleadingly at me as he asked, "May I have more?"

"Tomorrow, my son."

Unable to provide for the growth of our son's body, we at least could provide for the growth of his mind. Paul gave him instruction in math, science, and history. We hesitated at explaining current events, and our self-imposed censorship continued. We didn't dare air our opinions in the village because we didn't know exactly where that would lead. To be realistic, it was too late for others to denounce us to Nazi officials. Still we were probably surrounded by Nazi sympathizers who would call us traitors.

The elderly in the tumble-down house next door were so close that it seemed we were practically living together. Fritzi couldn't help overhearing them talk, and he increasingly became more curious about the war.

Neighbors Herr and Frau Broch were the most outspoken. Her voice matched her dark, piercing eyes, which were quite prominent because she pulled iron gray hair back into a tight bun. With a hoarse voice that came from deep within her where all was frost she questioned Fritzi with staccato emphases and quick pauses that thoroughly frightened him.

"Was your father a Party member?"

She extended her bony long chin toward the child.

"No, Frau Broch."

Even though she was old, her back was erect, making her appear much younger than her husband. He had obviously lost a great deal of weight because his flesh hung loose on his arms and jaw. Dirty gray hair matched the stubble on his chin and neck. Puffy lips. Missing teeth.

"Did your mother belong to the Women's Corps?"

"No Frau Broch."

"You seem to be a good boy. Did you want to join the Nazi youth movement?"

"I don't know what it is."

I approached the group just as Herr Broch was telling Fritzi how much he wished he were younger, so that he could be an SS trooper or a policeman.

"I was very strong all my life. When I was a boy your age, nobody could shove me around. I could take care of myself and of anybody who threatened me. Several times men came at me with knives, but I could always beat them up. If you don't believe me, just look here, son. I can show you the knife scars."

"Ach, another Hermann," I thought.

He began rolling up his sleeve for proof, but I interrupted, saying that it was time for Fritzi's lessons. Herr Broch must have been a bully, like many of the men who went into the SS or police. I preferred that all of us keep our distance from him and his wife, the old crone. Her suspicious eyes were ever watchful, darting from place to place, from person to person, like a hummingbird.

Paul and I didn't like to get into long conversations with any of our neighbors, though we knew the importance of maintaining some rapport. The Brochs were the most critical and very inquisitive.

"Why did you stay behind, Herr Merkel?"

"With a wife and child to care for, why didn't you flee west?"

"Why didn't you join the army?"

"Why did you think your family would be safe when the Russians arrived?"

Paul attempted a brief response. They told him that those who fled were deserters of the Fatherland.

"Did you try like a true patriot to defend your family against the troops?"

Often Herr Broch's sister, the widow Schuler, joined them. She liked to talk to Fritzi about the importance of obedience to authority, a virtue of the German people. I heard her.

"Tell me, Fritzi, why do you suppose the police have to discipline some people?"

"I don't know."

"Because they refuse to discipline themselves."

"What do you suppose was an important job for the Nazi Party?"

"I don't know."

"To restore order. Order! The Party had to bring a new order. Now tell me, what important thing is der Fuhrer doing for our country?"

"I don't know."

"He's restoring for our Fatherland the glory we lost in the last war. For a smart little boy, you certainly are poorly educated. Go home now. I've had enough."

Fritzi listened to her but told me privately that he always felt a zoo animal was talking to him because of her bushy eyebrows and the black circles around her eyes. Her gnarled hands reminded him of a twisted twigs.

"With all her white hair around her face, Mutti, she looks like the panda in my animal book. . . . and her ears are very long."

"Well, Fritzi, you be polite to everyone and don't share your impressions with anyone else and with me only in whispers."

"All right, Mutti. I'm so hungry. May I have something to eat?

"Tomorrow, my son. We must wait."

Another inhabitant of the next house was a self-proclaimed prophet, Herr Roedel. We pitied him because he was on crutches, though occasionally he put them aside and shuffled a few steps. We also admired his grit for having completed the 8K trip from Liegenbruch, but what choice did he have? Usually he was grouchy, but we overlooked his disposition in consideration of the pains he must have been experiencing. His head was rather large in proportion to his body; we were especially aware of it due to his frequent and loud pronouncement: "Hitler will save us! He makes us proud to be Germans!"

His wife adhered to the Nazi doctrine as firmly as he did. Wrinkled skin on her face had dried up so much that it couldn't stretch enough to form a smile over her rotting teeth. I especially mistrusted her with her thin, pursed lips that looked as if she had just sucked a bitter lemon. Her skinny fingers resembled chicken feet and usually were intertwined as if part of a straw basket. Each time she spoke to me, she moved the finger mass backwards and forwards from her wrists. The motion stopped when she was listening and started anew when she began to speak, as if somehow her hand movements were connected to her vocal chords.

One day we got onto the subject of dreams, and I told her one of my dreams was that every human being had shelter, food, and sanitation.

"Yes, Frau Merkel. Once our Fuhrer wins this war we'll be rewarded for our loyalty. He won't let us down."

She bent forward, stabbing me with her sharp eyes.

I replied, "But what if we lose the war?"

"Ach, don't you love your Fatherland?" Her pursed lips curled downward in an arrogant sneer.

"Of course."

"Did you know that Hitler has a miracle weapon? He'll use it soon, and then these Russians won't be able to rush home fast enough."

"They are making our lives a nightmare."

"I believe in dreams, Frau Merkel, that they come true if I truly believe in them. I dreamed that I looked into the heavens and there high above the clouds with his arms outspread to embrace us all was *der Fuhrer*."

"That must have made you very happy when you woke up."

Pathetic is the hope that infects the homeless who have lost everything and still believe that Hitler is their savior.

14 APRIL | SATURDAY

What pangs of mental torment Paul and I suffered. Suppose the Russians should move the two of us to a labor camp. Who would care for Fritzi? Certainly not the rapacious vultures that hovered around us. They would deny the child any scrap of food. I felt as if we were stuck in heavy sludge with these humans who had been robbed of their humanity. We endured every moment in extreme anxiety. Would Fritzi have to die?"

"Hannah, we are destroying ourselves with guilt and fear--first from the Russians and now from our own countrymen. Both the Germans and the Russians are denying our child his boyhood. His mind will be left with indelible scars. Already he is becoming more and more withdrawn, escaping into some part of himself that he cannot share."

As usual, Paul's analytical skills were acute, but what could we do?

"We'll plant a garden. It may be our salvation. At least it will be a symbol of hope and sharing."

So he prepared a small plot for our seeds.

"Even if all of the small part of the world we have known is crumbling, we cannot succumb. We have to continue as if we are going to survive and do what we can to achieve our faintest, short-term dream."

It pleased me to see my husband's more positive attitude returning. He was feeling he could be in charge of some facet of our lives, perhaps create some roots in our rootless existence. Ever since he told me about the "gift," my nightmares worsened. He thought he was preparing for a time so dreadful that we could not even imagine its horror. As a mother, I couldn't bear the thought.

After years of taking care of several rooms and spending my time on other hausfrau tasks, I was bored with rearranging our few belongings each day. While Paul was eagerly turning the soil for our future garden, I felt restless with nothing to do, so I decided that Fritzi and I would further explore our little village.

One woman down the road, whose name I didn't know, was especially hostile each time I passed by to get water. Very tall and erect, she wore her long blond hair braided and wrapped around her head. Without hair near her face, her features were all the more prominent: high cheek bones, long cheeks ending almost at right angles to a square chin, and a prominent nose with nostrils flaring. Really, she had the face and bloated lips of a horse. I never heard her voice but could almost hear her face twitch. The fact that she always wore the same dress didn't distinguish her from any of the rest of us women, but she spent most of each day sitting on a half broken bench with her arms folded across her chest as if pronouncing judgment on all that went past her. Why were all these people around us so ugly? Did their heinous thoughts transform their faces? Did I appear equally distasteful to them?

Living at the edge of the village, I didn't know exactly where some of the streets led or if there might be some accommodations better than ours. Obviously the former inhabitants were farmers. For example, a decrepit barn-like structure really was a dwelling, patterned on the medieval buildings in which animals were kept at the street level and the inhabitants had their living quarters above, keeping much warmer in cold weather due to the animal heat below.

Inside and outside these dwellings sprawled other refugees just like us. It was easy to look inside when houses were so close to the narrow road, wide enough for just carts and cars. Windows had been smashed out; doors were hanging on their hinges. Obviously some of the buildings were hundreds of years old and hadn't withstood the rampaging Russians. Where had the enemy sent these poor German farmers? Or for that matter, who was now living in our former house?

Suddenly Fritzi tugged on my arm. "Look, look, Mutti! I see the Grammens."

And right he was. I had assumed they would have been far from here by this time, considering when they left us. Frau Grammen was still wearing the flower-printed cotton housedress and green sweater she had before, both considerably soiled and worn.

"Oh, Frau Merkel! What are you doing here?" she cried.

Pleased to see each other, she and I and the two boys walked together through the village and to their little house. Her husband was sitting on the steps in the sunshine. I told them of our expulsion. They said they had barely started out of Liegenbruck when Russian soldiers stopped them and hauled them back to headquarters. They had no idea they would need permission papers to leave town. Arrest. Then confinement in a quasi jail. Herr Grammen again underwent intensive interrogation about his activities and those of suspected Nazis who might still be around. Only when the mass evacuation started, of which we were a part, were they released to join the departing throng. They were at the front of the long parade and fortunately found a house almost upon arrival.

Frau Grammen had cut her long brown hair to a short bob, and I noticed lines in her face that I didn't remember. She seemed in good spirits, as did her husband in his spotted and dirt-streaked business suit. Gone were his vest and necktie. He wore the same striped shirt, now wrinkled and grimy.

"I'd like to share an idea with you," she offered. "There's a small house, off the beaten track, just a few kilometers from here. We discovered some corn there. Come with us. Bring Fritzi. You need to get out of this poisonous atmosphere, and we're certain you could use the food."

"Oh, yes!" I exclaimed. My spirits were down in spite of Paul's nascent optimism, and I so welcomed upbeat friends and the prospect of finding food.

15 APRIL | SUNDAY

Because of our late start on the excursion with the Grammens and because of the weakness of all of us, we took considerable time in getting to the abandoned farm. The trip there was not easy, at first along a road deeply rutted by the passage of heavy trucks and tanks, and later we made our own path, trampling through fields. We didn't want to be observed any more than necessary and hoped Fritzi's and Rolf's presence gave a semblance of an innocent stroll.

Finally the Grammens recognized the farm. And we found gold! Precious golden kernels. In our gleeful gathering, we lost track of the time and ignored the darkening sky. Home we plodded in drenching rain and slowed by the weight of our treasure. Recent rains had flooded the Anklar River, which ran from village to village in this area. Smaller brooks sought freedom from the flow and established their own identity, like the stream in Liegenbruck. Due to so much precipitation, the broken asphalt road was partially flooded, and we had to slush along through the puddles.

It was dark when we approached the village. I hated being late, knowing Paul would be worried. For the first time in longer than I could remember I would prepare a good meal for him and Fritzi. The Grammens and I parted ways a short distance from their cottage. The area in which they lived was northwest of our little shed. Not wanting to arouse suspicion were I to walk through the whole village, I hugged the perimeter with my cache.

Fritzi was very tired and I felt guilty for having made him walk so far, but I had no choice. If I hadn't gone with the Grammens, I wouldn't have any corn. Paul probably was worrying about our long absence.

As Fritzi and I wearily made our way, a group of shepherds was approaching with a herd of cows.

"Good evening, Frau. You hurry not get wetter."

"Yes you're right. We're now on our way home."
"Is your son?"

"Yes, this is Fritzi. He's just turned eight."

"Eight! Small boy, tall."

"We've been evicted from our home in Liegenbruch, and he's not had nourishing food for several months."

"Hollow cheeks," commented one.

"Pardon, Frau, but you skinny."

"Yes, the Russians have little mercy," I responded, being a bit worried by this delay.

"These cows now Russian."

I could tell by their accents that they were not Germans or Russians. As if reading my mind, one offered, "We Yugoslavs, shepherds. Here, bread and cheese."

I found few words to express my sudden deep gratitude, but they knew what their gift meant to us.

"You come tomorrow, Frau. Bring pail. We give milk."

"Manna from heaven," I thought. I could hardly control my zeal to rush back to tell Paul.

"Oh, you are very very good men. May heaven reward you!"

I wanted to take Fritzi's hand to hurry him along, but my hands were filled with corn. And with the shepherds' gift. I dashed to the shack, smiling and laughing to myself, so thrilled with the food. But Paul wasn't there.

15 APRIL EVENING TO 24 APRIL

After putting down our treasures, I went to the house next door in the unlikely prospect Paul would be there. It wasn't like him to leave our belongings unprotected or that he would still be preparing a garden in the heavy rain. Then I heard the news.

While we were gone, the dreaded event occurred. The Russians came for Paul. Unable to scream, unable to shout, unable to cry, I clenched my hands in rage and frustration. Would this relentless persecution ever end? No one there could furnish any information. Yes, he looked depressed as they took him away. The Russians permitted him to take along only a coat, a bowl, and a spoon.

That afternoon and night it continued to rain as it had not rained the entire year. What madness possessed the Russians--and in such weather? I felt as if a bolt of lightning had struck me. What I had been fearing for months suddenly was a reality. Paul was gone, and I had no idea for how long or where or if ever I'd see him again. It is ironic how the winds of fate blow over petty lives from all directions, lift them with gusto, and dash them as quickly. At that time I didn't realize how lucky I was to have been away with the Grammens and Fritzi. They might have taken me, too. While I was relieved at having escaped capture, I feared for our future.

"Ah, Frau Merkel," Frau Roedel from next door surprisingly consoled. "Don't be so distraught. Many people were taken away today! They can't go far. I've heard that they're going to work not far away."

I imagined she was almost happy to convey bad news.

"But do you know where? Which way did they go?"

"That I cannot answer. Please, sit down here with your boy to rest. You look frightful."

I was scared, especially because I feared women might be called away the next day. What would happen to Fritzi? How he would suffer, completely alone. I couldn't rely on any of the vultures in the house to care for him when they had yet to give him even a kind word. The blitz hadn't hit them, and I couldn't help noticing how contented they seemed. There was a slight respite in the rain, and they sat in three chairs they had carried outside. In the damp evening air, they muttered quietly to each other, ignoring Fritzi and me.

In my dazed state, as if a ceiling beam had fallen on me, I had to think, to plan. I accepted that we were completely alone. First we had to eat, so I took Fritzi back to the shed, where we tried to restrain our appetites. Naturally I saved some corn, bread, and cheese for Paul, should he return that night or the next day, but I was pessimistic. It was imperative that I find the shepherds the next day to get milk. Perhaps they would give me an egg. Fritzi hadn't had an egg white for over two months. I knew I could get milk and eggs from the Russians, but the price! I would be reduced to prostitution. Getting food for nothing was like trying to grasp a shooting star, a faint far off glimmer disappearing in void.

The following day, however, I couldn't carry out my plans when a possible new danger alarmed me. Besides I couldn't have taken Fritzi and left our shed defenseless. All of us who remained behind were summoned to be examined for a labor pool. None of those taken the previous day had returned. Perhaps we would be sent to join them somewhere. Perhaps we would be taken away in a different direction and wouldn't be in Hilgendorf when Paul returned. The smirks on the faces of the vultures were gone. Herr Roedel was arrested, accused of being a Party member. The widow Schuler and two other women from the house were chosen and glared at me with envy when I was not selected. I was younger than they were.

"My child is too young to be left alone. Besides, my husband has been taken."

Deaf ears of the oldsters, shut tightly with the stubbornness of age, begrudged me my relative youth and my child. Ironically, those still left in the house smiled and congratulated each other because now their advanced age was not their misfortune but their fortune. If only I could escape this life, but I had to remain strong for Fritzi and for Paul, should he return.

Days went by and became a week. No one who had left returned. Each day we feared the formation of another work pool. Even Frau Roedel, who first offered sympathy when I learned Paul was gone, now shunned me for some unknown reason, even though her husband, too, was gone. I wanted to get away to look for the shepherds.

At first I stayed inside the hut with Fritzi because someone always came nosing around. The tedium of hours spent in limbo with little diversion scraped my nerves raw. Luckily there were no mirrors in the shed and most windows were either broken out, severely cracked, or caked with dirt. I didn't want to see my reflection: an ugly woman looking back at me: haggard, eyes dulled, greasy hair caught in a knot, cheeks hugging teeth. No wonder I wasn't chosen!

What to do each day? Nothing. Wait. Wait longer. A few brave souls planned to return to Liegenbruck with the purpose of retrieving items from their abandoned flats. They had no idea of what dangers they might meet on the road. Would the Russians let them by? Would anything still be there when they arrived? The Grammens were a comfort as daily we visited back and forth. Both of them wanted to return and said,

"We're so desperate here. We can't tolerate the people in our house. At least we'd be away from them and be together, whatever the risk."

A day later, however, Herr Grammen, his face very serious, had second and third thoughts and advised his wife to abandon the plan. His tone was penetrating.

"Every bone in my body, every cell of my brain screams to me, 'Don't let her go.'" He exhaled a sad sigh when his wife replied, "No, I'm convinced I could find some food in our house. Like Frau Merkel here, there are other women, a few with children growing more emaciated daily. All of us would go together in a band."

I felt desperate, more so than she, for her husband was still with them.

"I'll go with you. I'll take Fritzi. Surely we can protect the children, and they may provide protection for us. Heedless of guarding our few possessions, I asked, "When do we leave?"

25-27 APRIL
WEDNESDAY TO FRIDAY

Though we had little food, I packed a good portion of it to take along on our walk back to Liegenbruch. I didn't trust the greedy claws of the oldsters next door. Anything I left might be rapaciously seized. Hateful as those people were, I tried spending more time with them, being conciliatory. A woman alone in a shack was an easy target.

When we had first left home, I took nearly new underwear and stockings for all of us. My fur coat had been a godsend for keeping Fritzi comfortable. In fact, I don't think I overlooked a single article during that half hour's packing. I recalled how hard the exodus had been on Fritzi, and I wondered if I was being foolhardy by going back there and leaving the shed unprotected. Weighing the alternatives, I quickly added some clothing to the food package. I didn't want to take too much along, aware that I couldn't fill our little wagon completely on the return. There had to be room in it for Fritzi when he tired.

At that point, I began to question my motivation for the trip. Was I curious about the state of our home? Did I feel the need for bonding with other mothers? I never had been a joiner. Or did I simply need to break the tedium of monotonous days of waiting for Paul to return? Was I afraid of being taken away on a work detail? I didn't know. Probably all of the above. Life in limbo was taxing.

What a brave little trooper Fritzi was! How proud Paul would have been! The walk back to Liegenbruch was arduous, but I found our house nearly as it was when we left. I grabbed extra clothing for all three of us, especially pants, in the two days we were there.

On the way back, Fritzi commented, "Mutti, this cart is very special for us. It carries our food and clothing and me! I think it should have a name."

"Do you have one in mind?" I asked."

"Well it rumbles along in the road making noises like in the poem about the King of Persia, *Die Musik Kommt.* Why don't we call it "Bum Bum," like the sound in the poem?"

"I think you have a good idea. We'll make it official when all three of us together can name it."

As we continued toward home on the rough road, I actually heard the "bum bum" of the cart. But what a shock when we arrived!

The Russians had been demonically pillaging. Everything but a few stained and torn garments was gone. The intensity of my despair was alleviated only by the blessing that they had not taken the remaining food. They had enough of their own and better. I was inconsolable. How could I make do now with so much stolen? It would have been more humane had they simply shot us dead for practice as if we were some animals running through a forest. If only Paul were here, but I was forced to take charge of our lives now. The robbery gave me strength.

I began to feel happy that I'd gone back for a few items, though the price paid for them in stolen goods was high. During the two days of our absence not one prisoner had returned. To keep my sanity I had to ignore the wildest rumors that buzzed through the village like stirred hornets. Each report was a painful sting.

A new band of Russian soldiers had arrived during our short absence. No woman was safe. From the next house a 50-year-old woman was dragged out and raped on the ground in full sight. Were we the booty of war to be treated like the family linens taken from homes and tossed in the muddy streets? Conferring, Frau Grammen and I concluded we must flee a short distance to Augenfeld, where her parents had a small farm. We might find refuge from the Russians there and be away from people in this village. We'd leave as soon as Paul returned.

One escapee from the work force came back, Herr Klinger. At least he could tell everyone where he had been until recently but not how the others had fared. I immediately knew what I had to do. Surprisingly, I was daily feeling greater strength in having to be in charge. I'd always relied on Paul to make decisions. Now the burden was on me. I went to the Russian commandant.

"Bitte, sir. I wish to take my son and go to my husband. I can work along with him. You need workers."

I didn't know how he could refuse my request, but he did. I was determined to be with my husband, to die with him if need be.

Up until now mine had been the "unexamined life." Relying on Paul for every sort of protection, for food, for advice, I had lived from day to day as an appendage. I took for granted a secure relationship. Now I was jolted into the realization we had more than companionship, were more than colleagues in the lab. He had always loved me in his own way, I knew. Now when I was willing to die with him, I ached to feel his touch. Those blue eyes watching me with affection might never open again. I lay on a pile of straw, shaking with dry sobs. I couldn't let Fritzi see his only prop in these gusts of travail was becoming like a branch weighed down from winter's wet snow. The flux in our fortunes had to end.

1-4 MAY | TUESDAY TO FRIDAY
15-30 APRIL
(PAUL'S EXPERIENCE)

"Frau Merkel, Come, come. Some men have come to the village. I think I saw your husband with them."

Electrified with hope, I grabbed Fritzi's hand and raced to the official headquarters just as a motley group staggered to the same destination. It took us only 10 minutes. There I saw Paul--a hopeless bent skeleton. Dirty men wore tattered pants, were unshaven, looked like hobos. My courage sank in spite of the heavenly joy that shone from his eyes when he saw me. He took me in his skinny arms in a febrile embrace. We couldn't speak. Words were beyond us.

Fritzi, embarrassed, stood nearby. His father was not recognizable as the hero he knew. Slowly we made our way back to our shed. Along the way, I told Paul of our return with the corn, of meeting the shepherds, the trip back to Liegenbruch, all the things that happened on the day he was taken.

Paul was deliriously happy to be back at the little shed. It seemed to both of us he'd been away half a lifetime. He collapsed on pile of straw and cried himself to sleep. He barely stirred for three days, didn't complain or moan with pain, but his silence told much. He was tormented by the thought that we couldn't continue as we had. Having lost considerable weight, he was very weak.

I knew it had taken all of the energy he could gather just to get back to us. Besides, his ashen face and feeble frame, even his hands, betrayed his suffering. They were deeply cracked, like heavy soil that has been drenched by rain and then immediately parched by hot sun. The former stubble on his chin had grown into a dirty beard.

He began sitting quietly outside, content with our usual small portions, which were so much more food than he had been receiving. On the fourth day he felt stronger and began to tell me what he had endured.

"From the village 471 of us were taken; women were herded together. Very few men remained. Although most women were sobbing, the loudest cries were of those who were separated from their children.

"Oh, Hannah. I thanked the good Lord you were not at home. I know they would have taken you, leaving Fritzi to the mercy of our neighbors. He could expect no special kindness from them."

"Yes, they're already envious of him as we deprive ourselves to feed him. Go on, Paul."

"The march away from the village began just after the last glow of twilight. Because it had rained and was dark, we could not see as we splashed through muddy puddles and fell into the slush. Many wore only light shoes and were dismayed when the soles separated from the tops. The shoes of others stuck in the slime. Eventually, wearily, those people trudged on, barefoot.

"After walking about 10 kilometers, some women weakened. Russians sorted out the strongest persons to drag the weakest, but the strong were so debilitated by hunger that they couldn't continue. Time out was for only a short rest. The skies poured without respite. Not a dry thread remained on anyone's body. No one spoke as they stood still, for sitting down on the ground was out of the question."

"Oh, yes, dear. I remember the rain was torrential."

"We had hardly stopped before they commanded us again, 'Forward! Forward*! Schnell! Schnell!'*

"We were a bedraggled group and had to cover a total of 20K before the Russians let us stop for the night, several hours past midnight. The road on which we staggered was an old one, unpaved, of course. It was uneven, worn down by decades of erosion, its ruts deepened by wagons and cars and most recently by tanks. Finally we arrived in Barschdorf, so weary. I wondered if ever again I would see a town or a village as pleasant as where our own home was.

"The Russians provided shelter in two houses for the 471 of us, 26 people per room. Even the hallways were packed. As to be expected, each exhausted person had a choice in deciding how to spend this rest period: by standing or by squatting. In the absolute darkness I could feel glass and porcelain beneath my feet and could not clear a space to squat. Everyone around me found debris under foot, especially dangerous for those bereft of their shoes.

"While all of us wanted to shed some dripping clothing, there was no room to extend our arms enough to take off anything. I contented myself as well as I could in my cramped space. Every half hour I shifted positions. Oh, to stretch out for a few hours, or just an hour, or even a quarter of an hour, full-length, arms and legs extended! Devoid of hope, I prayed for oblivion because I knew a prayer for sleep could not be answered. I did not have one minute without sorrow, without remorse for the decision I had made not to leave in time. I would eagerly have exchanged my life for yours, should you still be alive. Each room was transformed into a pool of rain water. And so we passed the few hours until 04:00.

"Up! Up! Forward, forward!" shouted the guards again. Their eyes shot contempt at us. We were so tired that no one had the energy to move a limb, let alone to walk. The Russians had plans for us prisoners. Once herded into the street, each one of us received a spade or a hoe. What we would have to do or where we would have to go was not for us yet to question.

About 20 people could not stand up and did not get out of the house right away. They endured harsh kicks and clubings and were left behind in one of the two houses while the rest of us staggered through the street, weighted down by wet clothing and shivering from a chilling wind. By dawn we came to a halt.

"Our captors became surveyors, marking out sections 13 feet long. Each person had to dig a hole 1.1 m. wide at the top, .90 m. wide at the bottom, and 1.8 m. deep. I figured that the day's effort would amount to moving about 7 cbm. of earth or about 350 hundred weight."

"I am so exhausted, Paul, just hearing you tell what you suffered." I could feel the tears running down my face.

"That was just the beginning, Hannah. From those hours when the first glimmer of day appeared until dark when vision was impossible, everyone dug. Only a 20-minute noon break brought any relief. All of us were unaccustomed to such labor. No opportunity to sit down. No chance to stop for a moment. A supervisor, whip in hand, made sure there were no lazy laggards.

"Fortunately, as the ditch deepened, a few of us could rest out of sight of the guard, who had to watch over 20 people. Such respites were very brief because we had to accomplish the assigned task, so much earth to dig. Several people in my unit could not finish, and I barely had the strength to complete my own excavation. The iron disciplinarians steered the weak workers to a stable for the rest of the day and night, where they had to stand in water for the long dark hours."

"Such treatment is inhuman. Those Russians are savages."

"It was not just Russians. They were the ones who had planned the capture and assembling of our work force, the march to the site, our lousy lodging, the digging assignments, but who were the guards with whips? Poles!"

Astonished, I asked, "Had the Polish army joined the Russians? Were those Poles prisoners of war? Or conscripted workers? Or Communist volunteers?"

Poland had been overrun for centuries from east and west. Its borders changed with each new foreign invasion. As a country it hadn't existed on the map since the late 1700's. The Germans who had lived in the area for generations were Prussians. Russians had lived in another part of old Poland, and Austria also received her share. Due to the war and an identity since 1923, the Poles had a resurgence of nationalism, and armed with whips, they were taking revenge for territory their ancestors lost.

My husband went on. "By ten o-clock at night, those of us who had survived the trials of the arduous day returned to the two village houses, our temporary prisons. We craved food after so many hours, and what came? Watery potato soup and a thin slice of bread. Our lunch had been half an ounce of meat in hot water per person. Obviously their goal was our eventual starvation by the time we completed the work. And starve we did, day by day, unless we chose not to eat and kill ourselves.

"At first the suicides did not know the effect of their desperate act on us survivors, who had to bury them during the five-hour sleep period, from 22:00 to 03:00.

"We captives had no conversations among ourselves. No one had even the energy to groan. Names were unnecessary. Who cared who anyone was? Where have you come from? What did you do earlier in life? Have you a family? When the hope of keeping alive was the weak seam in a threadbare shirt, we couldn't think of anything further than enduring the next five minutes of toil.

"In very little time the health of all of us prisoners broke down. We could no longer endure the potato meals. Dysentery rampantly attacked everyone in the two houses. Our captors provided no toilets. The fecal discharges dispersed their own indescribable odors that induced vomiting up the little food which remained in our stomachs."

"I don't know how you survived. What a miracle!"

"Yes, Hannah, there are miracles. In spite of our deprivations my faith in mankind was momentarily restored. Our work force now was less than half the size it was to start. At least we could then lie down at night to rest. Near me lay the 40-year-old wife of the bank director, Herr Kreidler. She always had been a beauty. I hardly recognized her with hair short and stringy from neglect, but it still framed a face with delicate smooth skin and the kindest eyes I had ever seen, like an angel's. I was amazed by her iron self-discipline, obstinate courage. She not only had been able simply to endure hard labor but also had endured it with her femininity still intact.

"Work for her was strenuous in the Russian kitchens, as was serving us prisoners. Call her sneaky. Call her clever. Call her devious. She successfully stashed in her ragged clothing rations the enemy had hidden away. Secretly she shared these snacks with the sickest of us. Every person in our room loved Frau Kreidler, and every person would have made the greatest sacrifices just to please her."

"I wonder if I ever will see her again somewhere to thank her for keeping you alive and helping you to get back to me."

"Miraculously I survived yet another short night. A new day of work offered no moments for daydreams, only more immeasurable weariness. But let me tell you about Herr Kadow. That day I again worked next to him. He had been a farmer before being taken. A large man, about my height, but more muscular with the sinews of Hercules from years of labor in the fields. Obviously his square frame had once born more flesh. His somewhat darker complexion probably was not the result of working in the sun since it was still winter but from his ethnic background, perhaps Slavic. He'd moved to Silesia from the Posen area because his wife did not want to be far from her parents, who needed help on their large farm."

"It sounds as if you were feeling somewhat better."

"We two formed a pleasant relationship in spite of our different backgrounds. He was the first person with whom I had conversed, but digging side by side encouraged talk. His two brothers-in-law had been killed in the First World War just as your brother, Hannah."

"How old a man was he?"

"Like me, older than 50, but his very black hair had not started to gray. One day he complained, 'Herr Merkel, I'm half delirious. If I don't get a morsel of meat soon, I know I'll die.'

"I believed the man when I listened to his serious tone and looked at his haggard face. He asked, 'Are you willing to take a risk with me?'

I had already given up all claims to a continued existence at any level, so I readily assented.

"Here's what we do'," Kadow explained. "Just beyond our trench here, about 200 meters away, lies a dead pig. Shot in the head."

I asked, "What do you propose?"

"I propose that tomorrow we secretly crawl out there to get it."

His bright eyes gleamed with the mischief of a pícaro.

"Wasn't that really foolhardy of you two because you could easily have been shot, or did they shoot at you?"

"We did nothing that day, but I agreed to help him, and strangely, I slept better than night."

Paul smiled for the first time since he had begun this tale of two friends, and I realized he really hadn't had any male friends per se, only colleagues.

"We worked together the next day until about noon, when fortunately the Poles had become bored with the monotony of their watch and were no longer maintaining their former vigilance. The guards usually absented themselves to eat by joining some others at a considerable distance from us, and since the midday meal was a large one, they would take their time over it. They left their posts. No other prisoners were close.

'Now, Merkel! They're gone'

"Even though the guards were gone, we two fell to the ground, flattening our bodies as if crawling under barbed wire. It took little time to reach the trench, and even before we got there, I could smell the rotting flesh. We were nearly overcome by the stench of the pig and the sight of maggots crawling over it.

'Ach, Herr Kadow. You are insane in your delirium for meat. This pig must have been lying here several weeks.'

'The rot is only on the outside. If we cut off the hams and peel the skin, we'll find the inside is still edible.'

Kadow chuckled to himself, so pleased with his prank and eager for meat. The incident reminded me of when I found the rotting chicken and the magic you performed in the kitchen. At that point I had nothing to lose.

'Herr Merkel, just help me drag his carcass back to my trench. I can cut it up there.'

Crawling back to the trenches wasn't as easy as leaving them due to the dead weight. We inched forward in a single file, digging with our elbows, whispering the signal for one to pull and one to push. Once reaching his trench, Kadow grabbed the hind hoofs. In spite of his bowed legs, he was surprisingly agile. I turned my head away, took a deep breath, and held it as he shoved the front of the body while the pig slipped into the cavity he'd dug.

"For once I was thankful for having an empty stomach because I surely would have vomited. Even the corpses I had found during the occupation of Liegenbruch hadn't decomposed to that extent. I half expected it to fall apart when touched.

"Surprisingly the guards had not noticed our absence. Herr Kadow approached the carcass like a butcher preparing a prime loin for his best customer.

'So you have decided that a roll of meat is still edible. What will you do with it?'

'I'm going to take it to the kitchen to be cooked for us German prisoners.'

"I had no reply, and later he reported the results of his mission.

'The officer in charge stopped me at the door. He had rolls of fat on his neck just like the prime meat rolls I was carrying. He stood ramrod stiff as a new fence post and glared at me with his mean eyes, full of suspicion. I explained that I wanted to go to the kitchen, that I wanted the meat cooked for the German prisoners, that surely the Russians and Poles would not want to touch it.'

'Did he let you by?'

'He sneered, and I feared he was considering torture for me, but he said he would take it to the kitchen.'

"Later only a few ate the meat because it stank so horribly, even cooked, but those who consumed it didn't seem any the sicker. Probably their digestive systems had suffered so much harm that a little more didn't matter. I refused it, unable to overcome my nausea. I knew I was living in a daily nightmare, but I did not dare make it worse.

"Kadow and I completed the digging on our assigned trenches and moved with the rest of the group to an area near the air base, situated in the vicinity of a residential neighborhood. The Russians needed trenches for protection from German artillery fire that was close by. Moving about 22,500k of earth per person per day was the demand."

"How did you do it?"

"I was buoyed up by Kadow's spirit and had become obdurate in my new resolve to stay alive. Easter Sunday had arrived. Perhaps I could find something to eat in one of the houses. This was a time to celebrate Christ's rising from the dead, giving to the Christian world hope of another life, one beyond the grave. I was very aware of the religious significance of the day and transferred my hope of an afterlife to a fervent desire for a life after my near death at that time."

"The Lord does move in mysterious ways," I interjected. Even though we hadn't been church-goers, we had religious backgrounds and considered ourselves Christians.

"The Russians had gone under cover, so supervision was no longer so strict. The Polish guards disappeared. I closely watched the houses within reach of my trench. I saw a Russian officer leave. The moment was at hand. I would not only have to sneak to it very carefully without being observed, but also be fast in entering and finding something and returning. Off I dashed as quickly as I could in a stooped scurry.

"What luck! On the table inside lay three uneaten chops and the bones of five that had been consumed. Delaying just a second to make a quick decision, I took two and left one. Certainly the officer would remember that he had not finished his meal, but I doubt he would recall what he had left. I kept low and hurried back to my trench, where I shared the prize with my friend. Never shall I forget the animal ferocity with which we devoured those chops. You can't believe how good they tasted.

'Go get it,' I told myself.

'No, I might be caught,' I counseled.

'How good it would taste! I could share it when I return,' I rationalized.

'No,' prudence advised, 'Be satisfied.'

"I hesitated before stepping out of the trench, pretending that I had to relieve myself. A quick dash to the kitchen, throwing heed aside! The plate was empty. This time I sneaked carefully back to my work with mixed emotions, recalling the old Silesian saying: 'What you missed one minute ago no eternity will bring back to you.'"

Paul continued, telling me that complaints in the trenches had died down. Everyone was tired, like dogs that lie down in the shade to lick their wounds. Each new day was like the last except that their numbers dwindled and quickly were fortified by newly seized Germans to fulfill the quota.

Usually it was women who were missing. As to be expected, sexual assaults had not diminished. Every evening when the prisoners returned to the encampment, the Russians hauled out their victims, who often didn't return for two or three days.

He said he thought back to the time when the two young sisters sought refuge at our home, and he shuddered at the knowledge of what was probably happening now. He found slight solace in the thought that because of their inhuman deprivations, most of the women had missed their monthly menstrual periods. They were sterile. Their condition did not mitigate that the majority was still suffering from venereal disease. All were in poor health, finding no hygienic facilities to clean their wounds. Their pus-like discharge spread unchecked. The horrendous result was that the skin of many was eaten away down to their knees. A few grinned and bore the grotesque results of their rapes. Some took advantage of their disadvantage. They were promoted to female wardens and set up a minor bureaucracy.

"On the other hand," he recalled, "we spent pleasant hours with the young Russian soldiers who came to our home for meals and companionship. I am trying to reconcile those humane moments with the cruel treatment I suffered at the hands of these latest Russians. If any soldier was found consorting or even befriending a prisoner, he was shot on the spot. As were shot the prisoners with complaints that went no further than the commander in charge. The guards constantly sleuthed for evidence to take revenge on us.

"Occasionally a kind act surfaced only to be shortly stifled. I had earlier observed that a Russian first lieutenant inspected the trenching and noticed a Pole with a whip in his hand. The oaf was reprimanded; the officer snatched away the whip and did not notice the other overseers hiding their whips from view. Fortunately, the officer was not shot, but the whips returned. Then both whips and Poles were gone."

"Ach, they were treating you worse than animals."

"One day Kadow approached me again and asked:
'Have you noticed how the Russians don't seem to keep books? If someone dies or escapes, they simply grab the next person off the street to maintain the quota. I have my plan. I'm taking off.'

'Oh, comrade. How I admire your courage, your vision. But have you realized if you do not luck out, they might start a search for you? And if they find you, you will be shot.'

'You're right, Merkel, and I've considered the wisdom of what you say. But I've concluded that an end with horror is better than horror without end.'

"I pondered long and hard his words. Were I not two meters tall, I would have gone along on the next day, when some trucks were nearby. If we both left together, we would be discovered missing at once. Kadow carried out his plan.

"I was quite worried about my friend, whether he had been successful or caught. Not many days later, an overseer started questioning me about Kadow, several times, in fact, but soon he simply found another German and set his mind at rest. My mind, too, was more at rest when I became aware of how little the Russians concerned themselves with an escape. Kadow planned to go back to Liegenbruch.

"During that time my strength was visibly decreasing. I could tell I had lost considerable weight because my pants became looser and my jacket sagged over my shoulders. I began to feel my cheeks sinking; my cheek bones felt as if they were protruding like the tops of dangerous sandstone cliffs whose bases have been eroded by high tides.

"Still I clung to the hope I might see my family just one more time. Before undertaking an escape, keeping in mind the long walk back to you and Fritzi, I knew I would have to build up my strength. The most obvious means was to get more nourishment, especially protein. And where else could I find it but in the house where I'd gone before. One more time-- back there I went."

"That would be asking for trouble, even to be shot. I know you were desperate."

"I was lucky. The excursion provided an open jar of preserved meat, and it had been open for some time. It reeked abominably. Never mind! I was crazy for protein and wolfed some down. It didn't agree with me at all. By evening, back at the house where we were imprisoned, I was vomiting and developed a high fever. I wondered if my end had come. While others went to eat, I stretched out by myself on the floor, listless and exhausted.

"My angel of mercy, Frau Kreidler, realized I was suffering from some sort of food poisoning.

'Here, Herr Merkel. I've brought you some black tea from the Russian kitchen.'

"I looked up into her azure eyes. Her face was dripping with perspiration, but she was still an angel. I revived somewhat at the rich aroma. What gratitude all of us prisoners felt for her gifts!

"The following morning I stayed behind when the others went to work. In spite of being deathly ill, I delighted in the opportunity to stretch out full length on the floor again, alone in the room. But not for long!

"Kicks and blows with a club were the Russian prescription for a cure, no matter how high a person's fever. They made no exceptions for illness that would set back their schedule for the trenches.

'Up, up, you lazy German. *Heraus*!'

"I rolled to my side and with extreme exertion was able to raise my torso onto one arm. A blow on my back forced me to my feet. Staggering, bent nearly double, I left the house with a soldier on my heels, shouting: *'Schnell! Schnell!'*

"I don't know how I did it, but I had the strength to march a kilometer before collapsing.

'Lazy German. Take this!'

"Another beating and mores kicks followed. I passed out.

"I have no idea of where I was or for how long. I drifted in and out of consciousness. In my delirium I came to some sort of terms with my life. I had transcended my own tragic sorrow, envisioning my soul departing my decrepit body in a pillar of smoke, rising to the heavens beyond human hands. I would never see my family again. Hannah, you surely would have been transferred somewhere else, for labor or to be raped, or both. I worried about what would then become of Fritzi?

"How I had looked forward to raising my own son, only eight and so dependent. I prayed that I might see him and you, my wife, just one more time. In a burning fever my reunion with you came alive. Our former home emerged from my
delirium like a flower from ashes. If only I could be back in the wooden shed in Hilgendorf, be back there with you!"

"What happened next?"

"When I revived, I found myself in an open field, utterly forsaken by even my captors.

"What a perfect opportunity to flee! I couldn't stay where I was, so I dragged myself back to the house-prison. Miraculously I fell asleep. From time to time I awoke, with jumbled thoughts, although not completely disoriented. I knew my location.

"No medical help came. Obviously the Russians didn't acknowledge my sickness. I pushed from my thoughts all hope for survival or of your ever knowing what happened to me. In this pitiful state of mind I fled, hopeless, to my God, praying he would deliver me.

"Again and again I drifted into sleep, into vomiting. Unable to get up, even though I had the room to myself, I splattered everywhere. And in this condition my roommates found me when they returned at 22:00. My eyes were open, and I saw them looking in shocked horror at a dying man, so loathsome in his vomit."

Paul found out that, shortly thereafter, outside, with the headlights of their trucks illuminating the yard as if ready for an entertaining summer pageant, the Russians played on harmonicas and danced. Louder and louder grew their rowdiness and carousing in a macabre dance of death.

"Suddenly with three heavy detonations, the entire house collapsed. Debris whirled in a torrent, adding to the panic of the prisoners. In the dark, they tried to get free and succeeded only in raising their combined cries for help to nearly the volume of the blast. A German flier had noticed from overhead the burning headlights and dropped three bombs. But he missed the trucks and hit the house.

"I could not get up and run, so I fortunately was not trampled in the rush to get out. The room was on the ground floor. Not knowing what more might come, I moved as close to the wall as I could. Two splinters ripped my coat, but I wasn't wounded but too weak to free myself. I calmly remained lying there.

"Frau Kreidler told me that considerable time elapsed before salvage operations started. First the dead were carted away for immediate burial. Twenty-two of us wounded were being shipped back to Liegenbruch. But there was a mistake. I was not wounded. Consequently, I again received no medical attention. For two days I lay in the Russian barracks, ignored like a caged hunger artist. Fortunately Frau Kreidler also had been spared and relocated with the Russian troops, who had been pushed back some 20k. Once more she soothed my body and soul, at first with kind words and tea, then with bread, and finally with a rye pie filled with meat. My God had delivered me. My condition daily improved, but not to the extent that I could continue on the labor detail, even though the Russians scrutinized my height long and intensely before releasing me.

"Every vein in my emaciated body pulsed with joy. Freedom! Freedom! I wanted to rush outside, raise my arms to the sun breaking through the dark clouds and shout with praise to be alive. But I did have two concerns: one, would I be able to walk to Hilgendorf and two, would you and Fritzi still be there? After all, it had been three weeks since I last saw you. All kinds of things could have happened."

4-5 MAY | FRIDAY TO SATURDAY

"But those things didn't happen, Paul. You're back with us now and healing."

I had to suppress my eagerness to tell him what Frau Grammen had told me about escaping to their small farm. Paul was in no condition to leave, and I feared that the idea of going there and that it was nearby would start his adrenalin soaring and that he'd insist we leave at once.

Trying to build up Fritzi's and Paul's stamina, I stinted on my own rations. Each day I drank huge quantities of water, giving myself the illusion of having a full stomach.

I longed for a real bath! for a decent shampoo! Keeping clean was difficult with neighbors upon us and the shed barely big enough for sleeping. I couldn't completely disrobe at the stream. Oh, well! I turned my thoughts to being thankful that I had my husband and child with me, that we had survived so far. Everyone was in complete ignorance about the progress of the war. We had heard nothing more than the few announcements we got on the radio back in Liegenbruch before we left. It had been a year since some people were saying that Hitler can't win, more than two years since defeat at Stalingrad. The Russians were here in Prussia, but there were other fronts.

"Mutti, I'm hungry."

"Tomorrow, my son, things will be better."

Fritzi was always hungry. I knew he wanted to be smelling sausages frying in a pan, tasting butter and conserve on a piece of fresh bread. As bad as it was for Paul and me to feel constantly the pangs of hunger, we wept privately with pity for our child, who was wasting away. I sat looking at him and thinking: "My child, my child. What kind of life is waiting for you? Will you even have life after this ordeal? You're so young and innocent. I feel guilty now to have brought you into Hitler's world."

While sitting on the ground outside the shed the next day and trying to erase these morose thoughts, Paul came to sit beside me. He put his arm across my back, lightly squeezing my shoulder.

"Ach, Hannah. So good you are!" I smiled at him tenderly as he continued.

"All those days and many afterwards I puzzled how people could survive such torture. Perhaps because of the treats clandestinely distributed, few perished. Women were forced to complete the same tasks as men. What super human will empowered their feeble bodies to continue? Perhaps they believed that a heavenly force, God, was keeping them alive for a greater purpose. Suffering wilted my hopes for our future."

I looked down at his hands. Once they were immaculately clean and groomed. Their work was to hold tests tubes and to record findings. I now stared at dry hands, cracked with dark valleys of deep dirt. Broken fingernails covered filth embedded beyond removal. His face was half hidden by grime and stubble. He was alive, but for how long?

Paul suggested, "Now let's plan. We must flee at the first opportunity."

"I'm glad you feel stronger and are ready. There is a place we can go."

"Are you serious?"

"Yes. Frau Grammen's parents have or had a small farm across the fields in Augenfeld, less than 5K away. There's a house on two acres. Nearby is another small house where her sister lived. We can go there, the six of us together!"

"It is a reward for all we have endured so far, a Godsend."

"We know little about farming other than my having had a vegetable garden and caring for our fruit trees, but let's consider the farm a safety net, a temporary shelter."

"At least a respite from the pressure of snooping neighbors! Their only amusement is watching us."

"I'll go at once to tell the Grammens we're ready."

The Grammens had been waiting for Paul to recover and were anxious to leave the following morning, as were we.

Throughout the day we made several trips to their house. Not wanting to arouse the suspicions of the neighbors, Paul and I went separately each time, often accompanied by Fritzi. A bit of clothing, most of our remaining food--there wasn't much to take. Luckily their house lay at the very edge of town and in the direction we'd be going. We were so happy, so confident all would go well. To be with friends who had a son a little older than Fritzi would be good for all of us. Paul almost looked like his old self again--sparkling eyes, frequent smiles. Fritzi glowed with pride while listening to his father. How contented we were settling into the straw for the night, but those hours of carefree sleep disappeared as quickly as the circles Fritzi makes in a pond after tossing stones.

6-9 MAY
SUNDAY TO WEDNESDAY

Before dawn Russian soldiers tore open the frail shed door and took Paul away. He was to join a large group of Germans forming in the village center. Fritzi and I begged to deaf ears. All three of us pleaded that Paul had just been released from captivity due to his weakened physical condition. All to no avail. My husband barely had time to gather the few documents he might need before the barbarians started prodding him with their bayonets.

Once assembled, the crowd walked in the dark to a village 6K away. What possessions they had were taken before the men were pushed into a cellar. In all, they were a motley mob of 70 to 80 men, crowded so that only a few, the most weary, could crouch on the earthen floor. Paul soon discovered they had not been conscripted for a heavy work detail but for incarceration for their crimes. They spent the entire day in the cellar, away from the light, without any communication with their captors. And so continued the night. In the early light of the next morning Paul spotted Herr Grammen. The two men could not easily approach each other. Certainly they couldn't discuss the aborted plan for going to the farm lest they be overheard. So a nod from each in the direction of the other sufficed.

Existence was harsh. Only once a day did they get soup, and only once during the meal was permission granted to go outside. The frightful internment was exacerbated by rampant dysentery. The two friends once managed to stand by each other and to share their hope that after a trial they would be free again.

But nothing happened. Each night two or three were randomly extracted like trash being pulled from a bin, supposedly for interrogation. No one returned.

Divide 80 men by two a day. Forty days and nights. And no one returned. Long days. Long nights. Standing. Squatting. Starving. Grammen was called one night. He didn't return.

The guards called out, "Meier, Reineke."

No response.

More names were tried: "Salwasser, Hebner."

Paul called out, "Hebner," deciding to present himself. The guards led him into a small thatched room where two Russian officers and a female interpreter sat at a table. A petroleum lamp on the table provided the only light. At Paul's side stood one armed guard.

"Hebner!" shouted the officer.

"*Nein*. Ich bin Merkel."

"Never mind. We'll hear him," curtly proclaimed the officer in charge.

Paul hoped they would accept him. He relied on his intuitive knowledge of Russian behavior and his experiences since the invasion of Silesia.

The interrogator's skin was very pale and puffy. Obviously he hadn't been fighting in the field. His fat jowls sagged.

"When did you join the party?"

"Never."

"We know that 99% of the Germans were for Hitler, and now all at once no one is or was a party member."

At that moment the guard, crazed with hatred or power, approached and struck a downward blow on the side of Paul's head. He replied as quietly as possible with extraordinary calm, "I can prove it."

"Please do." He drummed his fleshy fingers on the wooden table.

Paul's heart was thumping hard enough to make his shirt quiver. Who knew where those papers might be now? He tried to explain his position. The officer yawned.

"We know the excuses. There are the scraps of paper," he said, pointing to a pile of documents on an adjacent table. Hundreds of German passports all looked alike. The task of finding his own overwhelmed Paul. He could only murmur as he approached the pile, "God in heaven. Let me find my passport."

He didn't trust his eyes. The seventh or eighth one was his, and with it the papers to prove he hadn't been a Nazi were still intact.

The officer again questioned him, this time listening more attentively.

"Here is a date, thirty years ago. I joined the Democratic party. I have been a member ever since then."

The interpreter looked at the papers carefully and made a note in her report. As soon as she finished, Paul took his documents and crammed them into his pocket.

They led him out of the building and into an enclosure with a very low slanting roof that was only 80cm above the dirt floor. The sound of groaning voices in German awoke fear and worry in him. These men also had been interrogated. Naturally they wouldn't confess to having been Party members, so they had been harshly beaten. Among them he found Grammen, lying in pain with a swollen face and broken ribs. The baker Turken's face was thoroughly mashed, almost beyond recognition, and he died a few hours later. Paul knew no one else, but he grieved for them all. The Russians were employing Gestapo tactics, but it was one thing to hear about them, another to experience them.

Paul knew the Russians wanted revenge, but they didn't have to assume that if a person stayed behind and didn't flee, he would still be allied with Hitler. What a paradox. The supporters of der Fuhrer fled to safety with their possessions. Those opposed to him remained, lost everything, and were beaten to death.

"What a lack of justice," he thought. "Fate plays no favorites."

Lying there in the midst of the groaning chorus, he was unable to philosophize further.

Suddenly the door opened, and two names were called: "Merkel, Schultz." Paul's and one other. He couldn't believe his ears and hurried to the door. When the second man asked for his papers, the guard fired a shot in the air. Paul had to get away as quickly and safely as possible. Next to the enclosure he saw three Russians set a shed on fire. He and Schultz started to walk away. More gun shots! Luckily the Russians calmed down and showed them the way to Hilgendorf.

The two men ran like children on their way to a birthday party. Before dusk Paul stood in front of the shed, breathlessly calling out, "Fritzi, your father is here!"

Paul and I sat down on the ground outside our shed.

"Hannah, we can't stay here any longer."

"You're right. The Russians could pick you up again."

"Give me two hours to rest up."

"Fine. I'll start getting things together. We can't take too much, but then we haven't too much to take."

During Paul's absence Fritzi and I had gone to the Grammen's house to retrieve the belongings we had intended to take to the farm. It was then I learned Herr Grammen also had been taken away.

"Did Herr Grammen come back with you?"

"No, only two of us were released. He was still in the basement prison."

Paul spared me the details of our friend's condition, and I was grateful not to know.

"Perhaps he'll be coming along in a day or two."

"In the meantime, Hannah, it's imperative we get away from here; we can't wait and must give the impression that we're leaving for a work detail."

"We know the neighbors will try to stop us or report us. They'll denounce us as traitors, and the Russians won't care that we aren't Nazis."

"They're probably afraid the Russians will take revenge on them if anyone is missing."

I immediately started packing. Knowing we would be away for a prolonged stay, I was more thorough. Paul fell asleep quite soon and needed more rest than he thought. We would tell our neighbors that we were assigned to a work detail and hoped our subterfuge would not arouse suspicions. The next day we were not ready to leave until midday.

Before we could leave, a group of Russians suddenly yanked open the door of the shed and announced they would take Paul and me to a distant work site. What irony that our pretense became a frightening reality.

"*Heraus! Heraus! Schnell! Schnell!* No clothing. No food. Out! Out!"

Fritzi cried loudly, but his pleas were ignored except that one of the soldiers let Paul run back to comfort his son for a moment.

Once again the center of the village was the gathering spot for about 100 of us. Men and women were not separated. As we approached the edge of the village, Paul had the presence of mind to whisper to me:

"This time these blackguards have little order. Run away the first chance you get."

"I'll try, because we can't leave Fritzi alone."

"I know these Russians," he continued. "They consider us a herd of cattle. No names. And Fritzi is not completely alone. We can try to get him tomorrow."

I hesitated, gulping. A cold chill ran through me. I wanted to flee, but would it cost me my life? The Russians had guns. Would they really take us back home at night? Or was Paul merely trying to allay my worries? I trusted his experience with the Russians, but I was a female prisoner now. Strong? Yes.

Taking the chance to escape was worth saving Fritzi. I don't know where I found the courage to make the attempt. Yet these recent days without Paul had completely changed my life. Were I younger, some might say I had grown up. Were I a boy, some might say it was a rite of passage. I made no attempt to fit my experiences into a neat box of slogans. I realized that I was a self-reliant woman that I might have to continue my life as a widow and mother instead of as a wife with a husband. My child was helpless.

Our band of prisoners was too unwieldy for a few soldiers to supervise. We walked no further than a kilometer to the end of town, where all of us were packed in a large shed, like cattle on a train enroute to market. What an uproar of cries and complaints! Paul devised a plan.

"This shed is near the Grammen's. Remember the brook there?"

"Yes, I know it--bushes along the side and water about knee-deep."

"Go there the first chance you get."

I went at once to a guard and pleaded that I had to leave to urinate. He looked at me suspiciously and said, "*Nein*."

I ignored him and walked in the direction of the trench. Then he called me back and all hope soon died. Several German women went up to him, waving their arms and shouting.

"She'll run away."

"She has a child."

"We have children, too."

"It's not right to let her go."

The guard couldn't understand what they were saying, but he pulled me back, confused by the ruckus. I didn't know what to do. Then suddenly my answer came.

Light rain had been steadily falling all day. It suddenly turned into an icy shower. To take shelter, the women ran back into the shed, followed by the guard. He shoved half a dozen in front of him with his whip. Quick as a flash of lightning, I dashed toward the brook. With a leap I was in the middle of a ditch and sought a bush's protection. My whole body was quivering, first from the cold water and soon from fear when the guard came back outside to look around. He probably disliked the chilling rain, for he soon went inside.

From bush to bush I crouched and ran. In no time I reached the Grammens' house. Frau Grammen was so shocked to see me that she sat as if instantly turned to stone, speechless, with her frail frame immobile. Then she regained some composure.

"What has happened?"

In great haste I filled her in on our situation and also on what Paul had told me about her husband's detention.

I advised her, "You must flee with us a soon as possible."

"I'm very weak right now. I can't. I must stay here where my husband can find me when he's released."

"I understand, but promise you will go to Augenfeld as soon as he returns."

"I promise. But now we must let your husband know that you've escaped."

"Paul may know where to find me. It was his plan that I go to the brook. It seems only logical that if I'm not among the other women when he looks for me, he'll think I'm either dead or here."

"Nevertheless, we'll send Rolf to your shed to tell him. The Russians can't hold 100 local prisoners very long, especially since you say there are few guards."

The young Grammen ran quickly to our shed and found Paul staring vacantly in despair. He had aimlessly packed a few more items, but became so distraught that he gave up. After the events of the past few days he couldn't pull his frayed nerves together.

"Oh, Rolf. I'm glad to see you. Tell your mother to come here. I have to talk to her. I must tell her some terrible things."

Rolf whispered, "My mother knows everything. Your wife has escaped and is at our house. She'll be back here at dusk."

Paul went manic. He hugged the youth around the neck. He danced with him. He gave him our last piece of bread, which Fritzi was supposed to eat that night. Then he recovered and sent Rolf away.

There was no time to lose. Paul packed our cart and informed the neighbors that he had to go to the Russian commandant to get his wife back. At the same time he was going to request a work transfer to Augenfeld.

Of course, he didn't go to the commandant. He hid for about an hour in the bushes along the brook. Then with a smile, he returned and told the neighbors that the commandant had agreed. His wife could return that evening and early in the morning they would depart for the new work site.

Old Frau Broch looked at him suspiciously with disbelief, her deep-set eyes like two black olives.

"I don't believe you. Show me proof. In writing. From the commandant."

Her dirt-streaked face and long white stringy hair reminded Paul of my wet mop for cleaning the floor, but her thin lips showed determination.

Paul had not expected to be blind-sided. How could a fellow countryman be so mean and try to stop a man from saving his child? Nevertheless, he promised to bring a statement back with him. I don't know how he cleverly managed the forged document, but it was good enough for her. Perhaps Paul had discovered she couldn't read. At any rate, the result was that the inhabitants next door were convinced. Had Paul not succeeded in his deceit, I'm sure they would have called the authorities at the first instant we made a move to leave.

Frau Grammen had given me directions to the farm. It wouldn't take long to get there. We knew we couldn't go along the main road. We'd have to go through meadows to avoid being observed by suspicious neighbors. There was only one solution: we had to leave in the earliest morning light while all of them were still sleeping. Danger still threatened. We could be seized.

That night we barely slept, so full of hope, but hope dampened by anxiety. It took only a whisper to awaken Fritzi, and in minutes, unnoticed, we crept away. Little did we foresee that traversing the meadows would be so tortuous. The heavy rain had turned the fields to cloying mud. Difficult as it was even to lift our feet, worse were the areas where we were forced to lift and carry the cart. It took us three hours to cover the short distance and reach our first destination: the main road to Augenfeld. In even that short distance off a traveled road, we met farmers here and there with the same question: "Where do you want to go?"

The situation was precarious. If a Russian guard came along, we were doomed. In spite of the cold wind, Paul was perspiring as if toiling in 90-degree temperatures. His clothing was completely soaked; I worried he would become seriously ill. For all his bravura in insisting we leave at once, he hadn't recovered from his ordeal in the prison.

Once a few Russian officers overtook us in a small car, but they didn't stop for questioning. As we progressed toward Augenfeld, the corners of Paul's mouth turned up and his eyes danced as they had when we were making plans for this trip.

"Misfortune and luck don't come equally divided. Perhaps today will be our lucky day."

11-17 MAY

At midday we arrived and had no trouble finding the property Frau Grammen had described. It was somewhat off the main road. All the better for us.

"Mutti," Fritzi begged. "May I please lie down to sleep? I'm so tired. And I'm so hungry."

"Tomorrow, my son, we'll have more."

Huge piles of straw lay about inside the house and were a welcome sight.

"Of course, Fritzi. We're exhausted, too. All three of us need some sleep. After we've rested, we'll look for some food."

We didn't even take time to look through the house for comforts. I'd read that sleep unravels the sleeve of care. It wasn't only the sleeves but all the rest of the garment. I don't know where I ached the most. As we stretched out in the luxury of clean straw, Paul conjectured, "I believe this was the base of a Russian watch patrol."

"What makes you say that?"

"The straw that's left. Some of the cupboards and beds haven't been destroyed. I believe they would have done more damage or even burned the house if they hadn't used it."

"Sounds logical. For now, I'm simply grateful they left the straw. We must get some sleep."

After a deep slumber of several hours, Paul was up foraging in the garden and was thrilled to find a few potatoes and carrots. About that time Fritzi awoke.

"Vati, I'm so hungry."

"Tomorrow, my son, we'll have more. Look here! Your father found some carrots and potatoes. I shall clean them, and soon we shall have a feast."

We went into the rubble-strewn kitchen with high hopes of a meal, but I discovered I couldn't cook because the stove plates were missing.

Oh, well. We cleaned the vegetables with water from the pump and ate them raw.

Somewhat energized, I commenced clearing the rubble. We surmised that the Russians thought they might be returning and for that reason left beds and straw. But that was about all. They obviously didn't want any refugees to set up housekeeping. We'd have expected the broken dishes, but the savages left human excrement and dry pools of urine in the parlor. Kitchen cabinet doors lay on the floor, ripped off at the hinges. It must have taken more than one man to break legs from chairs. And why did they have to break the glass in frames that still held pictures, though most were slashed? We had to walk carefully around the shards. A cabinet door was useful for shoving debris into piles, like a plow pushing snow to the side of the road.

I was able to set up three beds in spite of their mattresses and springs having been shredded. It would be a luxury not to sleep on bare ground or straw on a floor. The less one has, the less it takes to satisfy. After a few hours toil, we soon were tired again. I had shown Fritzi his bed, and he flopped on it to fall asleep at once. Not much more time elapsed before Paul and I also retired.

Horses pulling plows for ten hours could not have worked harder than we did the following day. Trying not to attract attention, we cleaned one room at a time, starting with the kitchen and bathroom.

"We shall tidy up one room in addition to the bedroom and live far better than we did in the shed," Paul commented. "What is most important is that the Russian commandant not find us."

Fritzi's eyes began to sparkle again in his eagerness to help. He hadn't had anything to do for so long. In the entire community that we let Rolf and he were the only children I saw, though I knew there were more. Those other families, or rather their mothers, must have lodged together in an area I hadn't explored. I recalled many youngsters in ragged clothing fleeing westward through our town, just hours ahead of the Russian advance. Had those families reached safety before they starved to death? What would the young ones have done if their parents fell along the way? Who would care for them? Who would have the time for burials? What might have happened to us had we joined them? Undoubtedly there was little sharing and much stealing along the way. Circumstances dictate morality.

"Mutti, should I take this trash outside?"

"Where should I put it?"

"Is there a broom?"

"Should I get more water from the pump? I so like pumping water."

"Yes, I know you do. Anything pertaining to water always makes you happy, from your baby baths to sailing little wooden boats in the river, to feeding ducks, to swimming, to . . . "

I couldn't go on because tears began to well in my eyes as I remembered happier days.

"Yes, Mutti. I'll go now to help Vati."

Suddenly there flashed before my eyes a small child giggling in his bath, splashing water over his head and looking to me for approval. It was the same look that he flashed when he first lifted his head and chest by rising on his elbows, when he learned to roll over, when he slid on his tummy, pulling with his arms, or when he pushed up on his toes. His first
tooth. Oh, what happy days those were! Fritzi was well fed, growing. He would sit in the kitchen, watching me prepare meals and helping in his way. How he loved listening to my records.

"Mutti, it's a good thing God made Dvorak because he makes pretty music."

The polka dots on my dress were "drums with moons on them." A plaid blouse was full of doors.

Different times. We hadn't seen butter or lard for so long that I even stopped longing for a taste of fat. Fritzi had once decorated the kitchen with butter while I was outside hanging up clothes, and he said if my clothes pole were longer, it could reach into the sky and pull the sunshine down. We had bread to feed the ducks, leisure to sail little wooden boats in the river, and now ... now.... Back to my cleaning. I wondered when or if the Grammens would arrive.

Fritzi found his father outside, surveying a garden area.

"Son, would you like to help me plant a vegetable garden?"

Before Fritzi could answer, a Russian soldier approached the house.

"Where pass and documents? Residence approval?"

"I have none. We were brought here from Liegenbruch by soldiers. We had to leave behind our homes. No one gave us passes or documents."

"Refugees must official identification papers."

"How do we get these papers?"

"Go military office."

"I'll go there tomorrow. Thank you for the information."

Paul was pleased not to have to answer more questions, but then came a surprise.

"Tomorrow you go at 17:00 to horses."

Paul reported the next day to where he'd been directed for stable duty and returned home fatigued and discouraged. Since his ordeal in the prison, his frantic trip back to us, his work detail and escape, he had had only a day's peace of mind and a night's rest. He was very weak, but he couldn't avoid this work detail. There would be no compensation until he'd worked 14 days. At that time the promised pay was 4K of flour and a bone for each week. To him it was manna from heaven even though not much for the survival of three people.

Promises. Dreams. Day dreams in the sunlight. Nightmares to plague me in the dark. A tentative tranquility took over even after our initial alarm at the visit of Russian soldiers. We might have known they would come. Paul charmed them with his suggestion that we would work the farm. They promised to protect us in return.

Promises. Promises.

Our next visitors were Russian civilian police. In they stormed late that evening to arrest Paul. Again he insisted he wasn't a Nazi, that the soldiers had promised us peace in exchange for produce. Many military factions operated independently, not honoring jurisdictions or the edicts of each other. All official words are wasted when scoundrels want their way. They left, but we expected to see them again.

"I was not raised for such harsh servitude," he complained. "I am not accustomed to working with horses."

I had no encouraging words for him because everything he uttered was right. Would he have enough energy to endure such labor until . . . until when?

"My fellow workers are luckier than I am. They tell me that they lost hardly a thing. The Russians permitted them to stay on their own land with complete freedom."

"It must be hard to work next to men who haven't suffered as you have."

"One farmer told me that at first the locals had to supply food for the cities, but they no longer have that obligation."

"I can hardly believe such leniency from the Russians."

"Let me finish. Hear the rest of it. They were swimming for a while in butter and cream."

"Do you think you could befriend them and get some for us?"

"Not any more. Everything was taken from them. Their cattle were requisitioned. They think the cows were sent to Russia. These men were forced like us to leave their native villages and were transferred here. Just as we were transferred from Liegenbruch to Hilgendorf and people from Hilgendorf were kicked out as were the natives of Augenfeld."

"It's all so senseless. Did they have to put everything into carts like ours and go on foot?"

"Oh, no! Wagons. They were farmers with wagons and could load them with whatever hadn't been stolen. At least they had tolerable nourishment from their working of the land."

Paul was slipping back again into his professional tone. So far he wasn't complaining of cruel treatment that day. He'd had enough of that to last several lifetimes. It seemed so unfair to put a man of his age who was so weak to work with farmers who had tilled the soil all their lives.

Luckily the Russians to whom he was assigned were pleasant people. The sergeant understood that Paul was a willing worker but a completely exhausted human being. Often his assignment was lighter, for which he was grateful until he aroused the envy of fellow workers. He was in danger of being isolated in this new world of "every man for himself," such as we had already experienced. At times he felt as if he were back in Hilgendorf with the avaricious neighbors surrounding our shed like hungry wolves.

The farmers took advantage of Paul's lack of experience by playing dirty tricks on him. If he was told to harness horses to a wagon, they tangled the reins and the harness and laughed at him if he couldn't perform the task quickly. The poor man didn't know how to strap the harness. He'd never dealt with horses, so the animals knew that no master was handling them and acted up. I suppose the farmers were unhappy being away from their own property and animals and sought whatever merriment they could create to put some laughter into their lives.

In spite of his heavy heart, Paul looked for the good in life. His present job with the Russians was easier than digging ditches and burying the frozen bodies of his fellow countrymen. He declared,"I told the Russians I want, unconditionally, to farm this land. We need more than 4K of flour and a few bones for three people to live on for half a month."

I tried to cheer him: "Luckily for us some potatoes are still scattered in piles, and the former residents stored carrots and beets. With the little skim milk which the Russians supply for Fritzi we're doing very well. When I consider how hard they make you work, it's unthinkable for you to come home to plant crops as well. Fritzi and I can plant a vegetable garden."

It was already mid May, so I could spade the ground. I planted the rest of our valuable seeds, which we'd carried with us like a collection of precious gems. I hoped that the occasional hoeing would keep down the weeds. Fritzi couldn't help with the heavy work, and my time wasn't my own because refugees came.

"May we please have a section for a garden?"

Russian soldiers came: "Cook this food for us!"

My husband felt bad that the farming wasn't progressing as he had hoped.

"Paul, I'm only one person, a woman, with a young child to care for and with almost daily interruptions. I lose an entire morning when the Russians come."

I was very weary and sat down to hear the rest of his concerns or complaints.

"Ah, yes, I understand. This house is not nearly so out of the way as we thought."

"I'm afraid to leave Fritzi alone in the house, and I'm afraid to go outside the house for long. A lot more could be stolen. Keep in mind robbers came here yesterday."

"I know you are doing your best. This summer we shall have more nourishing food from the garden."

"Yes," I thought, "if I can get it planted and take care of it." I was on the point of a breakdown.

He continued, "Day after day on a diet of breakfast potatoes, noon potatoes, evening potatoes and potatoes and potatoes. I've always liked them, but now . . . ."

He ran his fingers through graying hair and continued his catalog of deprivations: "No luxuries, no coffee, no tea, no pepper, no eggs, no fat, almost no salt."

"But Paul, we have a house, a room on the first floor. I admit the house isn't as tidy as you and I like, but I can't do everything."

'Ah, yes. I understand."

"We have a well, even though the water is contaminated. I boil it, and it's safe to drink."

"You were quite resourceful," he complimented, "finding those large milk cans for storing water. I am amazed that you get to the village for pure water and that you can handle those full cans by yourself."

And so went our new life. How many new lives had we experienced during the past few months?

Fritzi broke the tone of our conversation by running into the house, as excited as if he'd found a buried treasure.

"Muti, Vati, look what I have."

In his little fist he grasped spinach. Smiling, I held out my arms to hug him saying, "That's green gold, or should I say green iron?"

The find picked up Paul's spirits, and his steps were light as a waltz as he started toward the garden that warm spring night. He inhaled the sweet air with rapture and commented that we were much safer here than in Hilgendorf.

That thought jostled his memory: "Hannah, something has been weighing on my conscience."

He measured his words as if making an important point in a lecture.

"I should go back for Mrs. Grammen and Rolf. I have been looking for her every day, and each evening I think, 'Maybe tomorrow.'"

"I've been looking for them, too."

"Grammen was my friend. I feel a strong sense of obligation to him."

"Where might the poor fellow be?"

"He was being held prisoner when they let me go. Could he still be there? I wonder. He was seriously wounded when last I saw him. I doubt we can trust the Russians to have cared for him. They are all drunk with duty."

"Do you suppose he was left there. . . to die?"

"I bring this up now because I was talking to a fellow I met on the road yesterday. He broke out after I left. According to him, all the prisoners were sent to Russia for five years of forced labor."

"Ach, mein Gott! The poor woman! Waiting every day for a husband who may never come back."

"I am happy to be free, but I do not know if I can call it luck. All this has taken its toll on me. When I recall my abhorrence years ago of all mobs, I still clench my teeth. All their chauvinism. So pitiless in their eagerness for war. So desirous of seeking vengeance. Be they German mobs or Russian mobs. Only their point of view is the right one. So relentless in an inhumane and predatory war."

He seemed to be talking to himself, not to me, or to be addressing an audience.

"Paul. you can't let yourself get so upset again."

"Where does the lust for plunder come from? Back and forth through the years. Poland to Prussia, Prussia to Poland, Poland to Prussia, sometimes Russia here and there. What madness drives man to extoll the value of geographic boundaries? Such insanity pushes aside all logic in the name of convenience."

I stopped listening. He spoke eloquently, but I'd heard it all before. Couldn't he simply enjoy Fritzi's spinach? Yet, on he went.

"I tried to point out the injustice, but only heard in reply, 'In the great political machine there is no injustice. Might makes right.'"

"You know that's all wrong, but why dwell on it now?"

"Injustice? Right? Every day has its unique consequences, and we cannot escape them."

"Does it matter, Paul, whether man has acted unjustly or whether he suffers injustice? No one said that life would treat us fairly."

To escape, I took Fritzi outside to work with me in our field. He had enough sorrow without having his father deepen his already dark view of life.

The next day Paul was ill. I wondered if his lamenting had brought on the malaise. As he lay in bed, he continued soliloquizing our predicament.

"We can't risk being genuinely happy for one single day . . . I don't know if I can stand the work another day . . . too much needs clarification."

20 MAY | SUNDAY

Paul's illness kept him from work for two days. Every hour I expected the Russians to storm in to force him back to the horse barns, and I worried he would collapse from further labor. However, they didn't come, and Paul was able to return to work.

The weather was delightful with plenty of sunshine and warmth. Paul learned that the Russians had distributed a small amount of meat and a few bones to each worker in celebration of May 1. Even though Paul wasn't there, they did give him a bone when he returned to work, perhaps realizing that unless he had some nourishment he couldn't continue working. The scrawniest dog won't turn away from the barest bone. I was overjoyed at the prospect of cooking our first soup in two and a half months. In spite of his depression, Paul rejoiced.

"I can think of nothing else but the soup. I already see the grease floating on top."

"It's so good to see you happy again," I encouraged him. "I just wish I had some herbs to flavor it."

"Oh, for a glass of beer with the soup! I dare not even think of it."

How human we were! At a moment of greatest good fortune, we wanted more.

Paul's long-absent smile appeared and spread itself across his face into a wide grin as quickly as the sun comes from behind a hill and suddenly commands the sky. His former personality began to emerge as if he were in charge again.

"In these houses are crocks of beet juice everywhere, and there is the turnip juice you found, Hannah. I shall thin it down and mix it with some yeast and let it ferment. We shall have Berliner Weissbier."

Caught up in his excitement, Paul continued, "Every home has fermenting crocks. I recall seeing in the debris of the village drugstore some different yeasts for wine making."

Even though he had worked all day, he ran from the house as if possessed. Within a short time he was back home with a small package.

"Come with me, Fritzi. We shall take our little wagon to town."

"No, Vati, we'll take Bum Bum to town."

"Oh, that is right. Your mother told me you had given a name to the cart."

Soon they were back home again with fermenting crocks. I laughed at his zeal, but I didn't believe he'd be successful. It didn't matter. To see his exuberance made me happy. Of course, he started the process at once. Due to his adrenaline rush, he barely slept all night.

Paul's servitude the next morning was almost a pleasure, so sustained he was with anticipation: bone soup, a little spinach, and beer in the making. At the 11:00 midday break, he flew home for the feast.

I wasn't in the kitchen to greet him. The house was very disorderly. A fearful premonition gripped him, followed by panic. He found me lying on the bed, sobbing without control. I screamed in agony. Perhaps Paul feared I had been raped or that Fritzi had been taken away.

"Oh, Paul, it's the same, the same! I hate them! Those Russians came and stole our soup. They took it away, kettle and all."

"Ach, mein Gott!"

Paul sat down on the bed next to me, holding his head in his hands. Though his grief was as great as mine, he tried to console me.

"Lie on your stomach, Hannah. Let me rub your back. Try to relax."

He massaged my back and ran his fingers through my short hair. Neither of us could say anything. I knew he was as torn as I with rage and despair. How we had looked forward to our meal. How long we had waited for a soup bone, for a little meat fat floating on top of a rich broth. The aroma was still in the house, nagging like an unkept promise, hovering like a dark cloud promising rain in a drought and surrendering not a drop. All of our hopes sank into a black hole.

"And, Paul, that's not all. Do you remember when we left Liegenbruch I tucked into our provisions a small jar of preserved butter and another one of smoked goose breast?"

"Yes, I remember. We always sequestered them into the very bottom of our cart."

"Those were the very last foods we hoarded, always moving them and saving them for the most dire circumstances."

"Yes, yes, Hannah."

"We always deprived ourselves, even when times were the worst."

"I know. Let us stop the denial. I shall get them."

"No, no, They're gone! The barbarians stole them, too!"

I began to wail again. Poor Paul. His hopes had fled with mine. For once we both had surrendered at the same time.

Worried about Fritzi, Paul called him to come to us. We could hear him quietly crying. I tried to fight intense nausea by sitting up. We were caught in the middle between trying to comfort Fritzi and each other. Paul's last courage had flickered and died in the cold sweat that poured down his chest.

How bewildered Fritzi was. Until now he'd been through the invasion of our town by foreigners, fires and bombings, pillaging, ransacking, and finally expulsion from the house where he'd known security since birth. Then came life in a shed, his father's forced labor and imprisonment, and, and, and . . . I had, up to now, prided myself on my stoic stance. I knew that in the waves of chaos I had to be his anchor. But now! Now he was seeing his mother disintegrate in tears and shrieks, completely defeated and out of control. I fell back again on the bed.

"Fritzi," Paul directed. "Sit here beside me on the floor." He put his arm across Fritzi's shoulders, pulling our child to his side.

Fritzi had stopped crying. I was so overcome by my own grief that I paid little attention to what Paul was telling him. In time the boy went outside, and my husband told me to sit up.

"Hannah, my dear, all is futile. Sooner or later we'll starve to death. Just picture Fritzi standing over our dead bodies, condemned to a long wasting away--and all alone. What would he do with our corpses? I can't endure the thought. My dear, let the choice be ours. Let us all die together. We have no reason to live any longer."

At this point he completely broke down. His sobs were quiet. His body trembled. I couldn't utter a word. We stood up and walked to the kitchen. He got three glasses and took the poison from its hiding place, "the Gift." He didn't meet my gaze but looked off and then dropped his eyes to the floor, as if by resting there they could escape what was to happen. His hands were shaking.

I tried to understand. For myself "the "Gift" didn't matter, but for our son? To destroy the life of our son, a life so full of possibilities. Would he grow to manhood? What career would he follow? What kind of woman would he marry? Would I become a grandmother? I saw him again as an infant, cuddled in my arms, feeding on my breast. Later came the preschool days, reading to him, telling stories, feeding the ducks. Both Paul and I tried to lay a foundation for him to become an independent young man, making his own decisions, exploring on his own, setting his own pace. And now to destroy him?

"Come, Fritzi, my dear sweet son."

I watched our child go to his father, his big blue eyes so full of trust.

I pulled Paul outside the door. Then he bellowed like a bull being stabbed by a matador. Quietly I pleaded: "Paul, you're asking me to join you in killing our son! We've rescued him from war. He's skin and bones now. I don't want to see him slowly die, a little more each day, but your solution! A final solution?"

He answered, "Hannah, let's be brave. We must first be sure that Fritzi is completely dead before we ourselves can drink. Let us go inside now. Clench your teeth and look the other way."

20 MAY | SUNDAY AFTERNOON

I screamed and threw myself on the ground, immobile. I felt the paralysis I've experienced in a nightmare. But I knew this wasn't a nightmare. Fritzi was slowly dying of hunger, but this new death would be final. Was Paul being brave or a coward? How could he know that something good might not happen tomorrow? Fritzi was a blessing, a miracle, the greatest "gift." But what was my husband doing now? I saw Abraham offering his only son, Isaac, at Jaweh's bidding, but no religion was involved here. Paul would call it love. Fear wrapped itself around me like a strait jacket. I was unable to move or breathe. Paul ran out and helped me back into the house.

"I can't. I can't. I simply can't give the "Gift."

He took the glasses from the table. I sank to my knees next to Paul's chair and laid my head in his lap, listening to him moan. I wept and wailed and couldn't stop. Fritzi didn't understand what was happening. In a weary voice he almost whispered, "Mutti, won't we soon get something to eat? I'm so very hungry."

Paul groaned again, "Tomorrow, my son. . . . No, come with me. I'll go begging to the commandant."

He took Fritzi by the hand, and the two walked to the door, to the road, and away. I relive those moments over again wherever I see glasses of water sitting on a table, when I see a hungry child. Paul was desperate. He meant well, but he hadn't carried Fritzi for nine months, hadn't endured birthing, hadn't fed him at his breast, hadn't spent so many hours with him for eight years. Did Paul really love us or did his love transcend my understanding?

As expected, he got nowhere with the commandant. Then boldly determined, he entered the Russian kitchen.

"Let me starve, but give the child a little something."

The cook looked intently at the two sorry figures.

"Yes. War. Skinny. Much hunger."

Then she mercifully filled a bowl with hearty noodle soup. "Bring here, the wife."

"Und hier," spoke up a Russian soldier seated at a table in the kitchen.

"Bread."

Paul was so overcome with gratitude and surprise that he didn't know what to think or say. His knees were buckling so that he barely was able to walk away with the bowl and leave.

"Danke, Danke, viel Danke."

When they returned, I didn't accept the invitation to go to the Russian kitchen nor could I go to our own kitchen, the scene of our recent tragic drama. Did I love or hate my husband? He came to me in the bedroom, smiling and laughing a little. He had recovered to some extent, but I hadn't. I thanked the Lord for sparing Fritzi's life, that is, sparing it that day. As hungry as he was, Fritzi shared a bit of his soup with me before I lay down to shed my exhaustion. How long could we continue like this, living from morsel to morsel, day after day?

"Fritzi, come here to Mutti. Lie down here on the bed and we'll rest a bit to save our strength."

He was tired, too, but temporarily satisfied with a bit of food. Paul returned to his job with the horses, knowing how easily he could let his depression overcome him and bring on a manic panic again, no matter how he disguised it with his calm demeanor.

We still knew nothing of how the war was going except that a German resistance was considered possible. On the other hand, it seemed that our war power was being depleted. We knew the Russians were near the middle of the country. But every day German planes flew a counter attack, and we waited for the leaflets dropped from the air. The same message appeared each time: "Hold on just a short time more. We'll be back to free you."

Of course, we didn't believe a word of it.

21-22 MAY
MONDAY AND TUESDAY

I saw gloom spread across Paul's face the next evening when he came home to find two Russian officers sitting at the kitchen table. Expecting some form of violence, he tentatively approached one, saying: "Sir, we want to do something for you, but please leave us the last little bit that we have."

In good German the officer said, "You've certainly had bad experiences already, but be calm. We are not going to do anything to you."

Then smiling, he offered Paul a cigarette. My husband was completely perplexed. I watched him sniff the fragrance of the tobacco and ease himself into a chair.

"Sir, we have no knowledge of the world today beyond this farm. Can you tell us what is happening? Where are the Russians? Where are the Germans? Where are the Allied Forces?"

"Have you an atlas?"

"Yes, there is one here."

"Good. Then I'll come back after supper."

We didn't know what to think or if we could trust their sudden good will after all we'd suffered. We'd have to wait and see.

A further surprise. The two officers kept their promise and returned--loaded down! They had requisitioned from headquarters rations for themselves and spread them out on the table. All was divided into two portions, one for them and one for us. I could hardly trust my eyes: two liters of milk, a whole loaf of bread, a package of condensed pea soup, a quarter-pound of bacon, and for Paul a handful of tobacco. We fell at once upon the food, not remembering the last time we'd had enough to eat at one meal. How Fritzi gulped his milk! After they had finished eating, the officers left for a short walk, telling us they would be back to answer our questions.

Again true to their word, they came back to open the book on the table. I don't know why the old atlas had suffered so much water damage, but thankfully the pages still turned.

"Berlin has surrendered to Russia. The war in Europe is over."

We were astounded. Over. An end of hostilities. They showed us on the atlas where the Russian forces had advanced and explained kolkhozes (collective farms), so falsely presented by the Nazis. How eagerly we absorbed details of the end of the fighting. One officer pointed out many German cities taken by the Russians and the Western Powers, who had joined forces at Torgau on the Elbe River.

But just as our own country had lied to us, were these Russian officers deceiving us, too? They seemed trustworthy, yet we had our doubts because just last week German planes continued to drop their fluttering message to hold fast, and we heard the thundering cannons in the distance during sleepless nights. But all had been quiet the past week. We thanked them for the food and information and went to bed quite incredulous.

On the next day the Russians came again, this time with a wounded man from a railway train. They took him for a sick German, but he really was a wounded Frenchman from Metz. He'd received shrapnel from a German bomber. Naturally he wanted to get home, but now he was forced to work for the Russians. Paul questioned him in detail about recent events and concluded the Russian officers had told us the truth.

"Thank God the war is over."

"Yes," interjected the Frenchman. *"Kaputt."*

He stayed with us only overnight, for the Russians took him away the next day to their camp. When Paul went to work, the Russian sergeant told him, "War *kaputt."* Paul still wasn't sure he could believe the news, so he asked others at the stables.

"Ja, ja, kaputt."

It was true. Paul felt himself out of time and space, filled with only joy at the conclusion of the senseless and criminal war. This was a great historical moment. Once again Germany lay on the ground, defeated. Pitted against her were the hatred and mistrust of the whole world.

I really can't remember if or how I celebrated. There was no physical change in our circumstances. We felt freed from a heavy burden we'd born, but into the vacuum it left rushed the inevitable question: "What next?" Surely after the ceasefire, the plundering and rape would stop. Could we return to our flat in Liegenbruch? Would the university open again? What kind of government could we expect? How would Paul support us?

He went to his vats, elated. The beer tasted outstanding to him, but homemade brew always tastes like the best. The important thing was his joy that day. As he quaffed a cup, he looked sorrowfully at the garden, commenting that spading it now hardly would make a difference. Or would it?

23 MAY | WEDNESDAY

Paul's thoughts were of staying on.

"I think I shall ask the Russians for a horse and a plow. If the ground were evenly plowed, we could easily plant potatoes in every second furrow. In this warm weather we could expect sprouts quite soon."

I was heartened by his hopeful tone, that he could even think the Russians willing to help us. But was he considering remaining in Augenfeld instead of returning to Liegenbruch? Of course, all was in a flux.

Early the following morning we were surprised by a knock on the door. The Russians usually just broke in, but recalling the many visits from looters in Liegenbruch, we dreaded who it might be. It was a woman wearing a peach-colored blouse beneath a man's shabby, shapeless cardigan. The sleeves had been rolled up several times to nearly where her bony elbows poked out. As she introduced herself, she nervously twisted and clasped her skinny fingers that appeared deformed by arthritis.

"I am Frau Kratz. This is my home. I have come back. I'm waiting for my husband. We lived here for many years. The Russians came and forced us out. We built this house and had this small farm. We raised our vegetables here and had a few animals. The Russians said they needed this house for the soldiers and that we must move. Who are you people and what are you doing here?"

She spoke slowly without pausing for breath. So much information. So many questions. I could tell from her speech that she was a farm wife. Although she was shabbily dressed and appeared somewhat malnourished, judging by the way loose skin drooped on her face, she exuded a certain strength. Stray locks of gray hair blew towards her face in the strong wind that had come up. I suspected that she might have worn glasses at one time by the way she got very close to us for a look, tilting her head to the right as if she could see better with her left eye. Obviously she once had weighed considerably more than she now did.

"Oh, you must be the mother of Frau Grammen. She's our friend and told us to come here when we escaped from Hilgendorf."

"Where is my daughter now? She must be about 40 years old by this time. She and her husband had a son named Rolf. They moved to Liegenbruch. He got a good job there. I don't know if he joined the Party. Perhaps he had to in order to get good pay. She was always a good girl. Both of my girls were good girls. Heaven only knows where the other one is now. Her name was Erma."

Finally I managed to answer her question.

"We've been expecting Frau Grammen every day. She didn't want to come with us because she and Rolf were waiting for Herr Grammen to return from prison."

"Prison? What was he doing in prison? Did the Nazis put him away or was it the Russians? What did he do wrong? He was always such a quiet fellow. Seemed nice enough. Responsible. Probably a good husband and father."

"Do come in, Frau Kratz. Don't stand here in the wind."

She teetered on a cane made from a sturdy branch. Although we sat down at the kitchen table, I had nothing to offer her to eat or drink.

"This is our son, Fritzi," I introduced, putting my arm over his shoulders.

"Why is my daughter's husband in prison? Who put him there? What did he do wrong? He's not the violent kind, so maybe he cheated someone. He was always so quiet. He never talked about his business."

"My husband also was in the same prison. Why is anyone taken away to prison? The Russians don't need reasons. They suspect that every man who stayed behind is a Nazi or sympathizer. Herr Grammen was still there when my husband got away. We have had no news since that time. Now my husband is working with horses for the Russians."

"Is he a good farmer? The Russians need good help."

"Oh, my husband isn't a farmer. He was a chemistry and physics professor. The Russians pay little attention to what a person has been trained to do if they need labor."

"*Ja, ja,* they want all of us Germans to be their slaves. Tell me about my daughter. You say she's coming here soon. Where is she now? When did you last see her? How long have you been waiting here for her? Will her son come with her?"

"She's well and with other Germans who were relocated to Hilgendorf. Perhaps she will come here any day now. Now please tell me what happened to you here."

"One night we heard loud rumblings outside. Like nothing we heard before. It's always quiet here in the country and away from the main road. The noises didn't stop. We became more and more frightened. We ran to the window to look out. We didn't know if we'd be able to see anything or not. It was no use to stay shivering in bed. What do you suppose was there? There were Russian tanks--enormous tanks right outside the door. My husband and I were scared. We decided to get dressed. We knew then that the village was occupied. My husband told me to put on an extra sweater and a warm coat. I thought I wouldn't need them. I didn't think we would go outside. We were just two elderly people, innocent. Well, we barely took off our nightclothes and they started pounding on the door. I thought they were going to knock it down. My husband told me to stay back. He went to see what was going on. We had to open the door to some Russians. They just shoved us aside, demanding food. At that hour!"

It seemed that Frau Kratz was like one of those mechanical toys that start up and keep going without a stop until they run down. Words just kept tumbling out of her as if she hadn't had an audience for months.

"So they could speak German?"

"Well, they kept saying *'essen, essen, essen,'* so we knew they wanted food. We didn't understand very much. All jumbled German and Russian. They kept moving their hands to their mouths and pretending to eat. We guessed that they were hungry. My husband and I went to the kitchen. We gave them good black bread, sausage, cheese. I boiled some eggs. And then before they ate they all said 'schnapps, schnapps.'"

"That's what all of them demand," I said. "Then did they leave you alone?"

"Oh, no. We had no schnapps. My husband's father drank a lot. He was a very poor provider. He spent his extra harvest money on liquor. Which he drank day and night. His poor wife never had a new dress. In fact, her underclothes were little more than holy rags. There were three boys. My husband one of them, the youngest. They were beaten every day if they even rested a little bit during their farm chores. The older boys ran off to sea. Just my husband was left, and he had all the worse beatings. He hated his father. His mother took ill with something that made her spit a lot of blood and she died. So the young boy decided he would never have a drop of schnapps in the house. That's why we had none for the Russians."

"I suppose they searched the house and found none and then went looking elsewhere."

"For a day, they did. But after that every day they came back for more food. They wanted me to cook for them while they searched the basement and cupboards. On the third day they took away our cows and our four horses. So we had no more milk. My husband wouldn't have horses for plowing in the spring. Our farm isn't big, but we needed horses. We were elders."

"You must have been feeling very angry and upset."

"Yes, we were. At least they didn't beat us or rape me."

"Consider yourselves lucky."

"Yes. Those men were common men and couldn't speak German. We never knew what they wanted. Always we could hear guns and fighting not far away. We didn't know if they were winning or losing. About the fifth day an officer came with them. He told us we had to leave the house in 30 minutes."

"It was the same with us when we had to leave Liegenbruch."

"We never thought that would happen. We weren't ready. What should we take? So I gathered some clothes and food and blankets. I asked my husband what we should do and if they really meant what they said. He just told me to stop talking and asking questions and just to pack what seemed necessary. I wish they had left us at least one wagon and one horse. There wasn't even time to think. He got a cart from the shed, and we loaded it while the soldiers watched and laughed and made fun of us. They imitated us hurrying around to look for things."

"How humiliating."

"Yes, but at least they didn't beat us. They told us to go to the road and move toward Kurzfeld. The road was full of people, just like us."

"Where is your husband now?"

""Ach, my husband! About 20K from here the Russians separated the men and women. The men waited at a crossroads to be taken to a work camp. The guards hit us women and children with whips if we didn't hurry. I didn't know what would become of him. They left me in a village nearby. I was staying with some pig farmers. I felt safe there, but I didn't like to see all the pigs killed every day."

"I assume you had some food to eat."

"There was very little for us, but the Russians demanded lots of pork."

"How did you get away from them?"

"Oh, they left to go west toward Berlin. We heard that the Allied Forces were coming, and the Russians went to meet up with them. They took all the meat along. The rest of the pigs they loaded onto boxcars to send back to Russia. You know the railroad is very close. It goes west from here through Kurzfeld. A few days ago I heard the war was over. I saw there was no reason for me to stay at the pig farm, so I decided to come back home. I hope my husband is still alive and comes home, too."

"When did you leave that farm?"

"I've been walking two and a half days. I have arthritis in my right hip and can't move very quickly. I have a lot of pain. On my way back here I saw nothing but burned houses everywhere. What a blessing mine is still here."

The woman was obviously tired from her long walk. She must have been in her late sixties and definitely showed signs of malnutrition. Her voice seemed to be giving out as her speech slowed. She sat still, quietly looking around.

Knowing she wanted to know more, I explained: "The Russians didn't leave much behind for you to come back to, as you can see. We've cleaned the house since our arrival. My husband thinks that the Russians must have used it as a base for a watch patrol. At least they left clean straw, which was a godsend for us after considerable sleeping on the ground."

"What a blessing the house was spared and that you've cared for it. All the way back, I passed smoking barns and houses. I thought I would find charred timbers here. I wept. I'm living with the hope that my husband will come back here to look for me. I wish they had taken me away with him. An old woman alone has so many worries. Only the hope of being with him again keeps me going."

"And where are your other daughter and her husband? Frau Grammen said she had a married sister."

"Oh, they went west at the first news that the Russians were advancing. They lived right next door to here in the little house over there," she said pointing out the window.

"She tried to persuade us to go away, too, but we said that we had nothing to fear from the enemy. We weren't Nazis or Party members."

In Paul's and my preparations to make the house habitable, we hadn't counted on anyone else living with us immediately. We planned to improvise when Frau Grammen and Rolf arrived because the little house of her sister had been trashed beyond repair. Frau Kratz's unexpected arrival was a surprise. Sensing her exhaustion, I encouraged her to rest on Fritzi's bed. All this while I had kept my eye on him playing the little farmer with his spinach plot.

When Paul came home at midday, Frau Kratz was up again and questioned him about her son-in-law, but he had no inclination to tell her what he last saw. I divided our meager rations into four portions, giving extra to Paul and Fritzi. We were glad to welcome her and for her possible help in caring for the garden, but heavens! How could we feed her?

We were close to starvation ourselves. Due to the war, fields had not been cultivated anywhere. Since the invasion, all root crops had been confiscated by either the Russians or by refugees like us. Most farm workers were still away. For months the corn, which had been rotting on the ground, was overrun by rats and mice carrying diseases. Most potatoes had been dug and eaten. Frau Kratz told us she had seen very few cows and that soldiers were guarding them. The rest of the cattle had been shipped back to Mother Russia. The poor woman was extremely distraught, but content to be at home once more.

Paul returned to work, still determined to ask the Russians for a horse and plow. Dubious, I hated to see him come home empty-handed and discouraged again. I was skeptical about his having any success.

24 MAY TO 9 JUNE

At sunset, much to my amazement, Paul returned with both a horse and a plow. Remembering that day, even now I smile with pleasure recalling the look of victory on his face as he approached. A smile was rare in those troubled times.

From his experiences on the work detail, he knew something about handling a horse, but he'd never held a plow in his hands before. However, his determination propelled him. Within ten minutes he had blood blisters on both hands and the nag had stepped on his right foot so that his stocking was plastered to his foot from the sticky blood. Beneath them lay a crushed big toenail. The poor fellow hadn't completed a single furrow.

About that time Ivan, a tall, muscular Russian sergeant came by. He had black hair and dark complexion. His square chin reminded me of the chins of much admired film stars, and a friendly smile put us at ease.

Immediately assessing the tragicomedy before him, he took charge. With pity for us and pride in being a farmer, he grabbed the horse and plow. In no time he completed the furrows on our plot. We three Merkels and Frau Kratz followed him, dropping potato eyes as quickly as there was a place to plant them. Paul's foot hurt him terribly so that he hardly kept up. It took all of us only two hours!

"What can we offer Ivan in return?" Paul questioned me. "We can't give him any food. Should I get him a glass of my beer?"

"We don't have anything else."

Hesitantly and not wanting to be ungrateful, Ivan held out his large dirty hand for the somewhat cloudy drink. Suddenly his face lit up.

"*Karosch*! (Good) More!"

After he left, Paul smiled again, with pride: "I'm so glad I found a way to repay him."

Not fifteen minutes had passed before Ivan returned--this time with two companions. Of course, they, too, wanted beer. Full of praise, one who spoke some German, likened it to a native drink, *Quas*, and wanted the recipe. After a few more beers, Paul's occupation was decided. He didn't have to work on the farm with the horses any longer. He would brew beer!

Unfortunately those Russians hadn't the authority to make the final decision. Paul would still have to spend part of the day cleaning stables. Envy infected his fellow workers, so they complained to the Russian officers, who explained that Paul was not a regular field hand but an intellectual, a professor. However, a complication arose in the reversal of his status with the Russians. Paul was unable to make clear to his captors that he didn't have all kinds of advice. He was most surprised that to them "doctor" meant only "medical doctor." In their limited experience with academia, a "doctor" was a "doctor."

One day they took to Paul a corporal who had accidentally shot himself through his boot, stocking, and foot. Paul said the man was just a boy, not a lot taller than Fritzi and with a similar shock of blond hair that flopped over his right eye. He probably had received little training in the use of small firearms and was visibly shaking with shock and pain. When Paul removed the boot and sock, the young man winced even further to gaze down at a horrendous, thickly swollen, bloody mass. Rather than incurring the wrath of the officers by insisting he was a teacher, not a physician, Paul knew he had to do something.

"Bring me some hot water and soda."

Hoping a soak in the solution would stimulate bleeding, he cleansed the wound as well as he could. Then he daubed it with tincture of iodine and bandaged it as skillfully as possible.

"I advise you now go to the Russian military hospital."

"No, No. I not to go!" the corporal protested. "They give me not food. My officer punish."

Knowing he had done all he could, Paul feared that if the foot didn't heal, he would be held responsible. What do they say? Fear is being afraid of something that probably won't happen anyway. It didn't. After three days the little corporal was running around again, and after a week he was quite all right.

Then the Russians really respected Paul. As he rose in their estimation, he was pestered on all sides, but dental surgery was out of the question. His spirits continued to improve; he was a necessary piece on the Russian chessboard.

Day and night the soldiers showed up at the farmhouse, throats burned with their own homemade "Schnapps." Hangovers. The right medicine was always Paul's good beer. They brought sugar, onions, and bacon.

We were delirious with happiness. Fat. How we had longed for fat. I fried potatoes so that they swam in bacon grease. The "guests" ate red onions by the pound, dipping them in salt. They invited us to join them in those meals that I was commandeered to cook, but after so many months of near starvation, we were disappointed that our stomachs could not support the heavy diet.

In no time, Russians from nearby villages came to exchange sugar for beer. Many days they consumed up to 60 liters. Under other conditions, Paul could have established a regular business, but his knowledge was limited to making beer from sugar and syrup. He failed completely trying to use grain.

Like children who have just received their allowance and don't know the virtue of saving or allocating, the Russians spent in abandon a month's sugar ration in ten days. At the same time the innocent young fellows wanted to pay something to continue drinking. Thus began our collection of useless minutia: bags, meat grinders, wire screen, money. The best payment was bread and flour.

A sense of order had been restored to our topsy-turvy world. We knew we would not be staying with Frau Kratz a long time, but in those days, we were grateful for even a few days' security. Fritzi began to gain some weight. With a lighter work load at the stables, Paul came home with energy left over for gardening. I loved seeing him and Fritzi laughing together as they planted and weeded vegetables. They could manage garden pests quite well, but not the next problem that was to descend upon us like a plague of locusts.

As reparations, the Russians had taken out some of the railroad tracks to send back to the Motherland. They left enough for the passage of a few trains, but not all. A simple journey the distance from Dresden to Breslau took 30 days. At a small, brick railway station close to the Kraus farm a train often remained from five to 14 days. As to be expected, passengers had no food and little or no baggage. The Kraus farm, so close-by, was an easy target. We assumed some travelers had found their former homes mere skeletons of charred timbers and were seeking places to "squat."

Like eager grasshoppers, passengers descended from boxcars and spread into the environs where they villainously stole everything. Paul and I had nothing left for them to pillage except . . . except our garden. It was ravaged. Our hearts bled at the sight of the devastation: cheery trees were broken down, beets and onions were pulled from the ground; vegetables too small to eat were left to dry up.

The vagrants trampled berries, still green on their twigs. Whatever remained was hardly worth the effort to rescue, but we had to eat. On the surrounding farms unplowed and unplanted fields yielded nothing for the hungry. Though it was only a matter of months since we had fled our own home, it seemed we had saved precious vegetable seeds all our lives-- for naught.

As quickly as it arrived, the plague departed like a tornado, leaving only destruction behind. Paul's "customers" at his *Bierstube* (tavern) also left. Their leader, Sergeant Ivan, brought us a farewell gift: a 40-pound sack of grits. We guessed the departing soldiers would be replaced by new ones.

The young replacements evidently had been informed of Paul's beer and came to drink it as freely as had the others, but in exchange we received only useless trifles. Paul was grateful he was still permitted to brew beer, yet the ingredients that he secured were quickly dwindling. He didn't want to incur the ire of the young troops by requesting sugar, and he found that language was becoming more of a barrier as well. Beer was Paul's security card for freedom from forced labor, but what would we do for barter when he had to give up brewing?

About that time a couple came to the farm who were quite different from the other *Flüchtlinge* (refugees). We spotted them roaming around the garden, just as on any given day strangers wandered there. We never knew where people came from, be they returning Prussians or Poles.

Paul and I were outside the house when they approached us. Before the woman had even uttered a word, her classical good looks and demeanor told us she was from the upper class. In fluent German she asked if she could pay us for whatever fruit we could spare. Five months earlier the Russians had paid for beer with sugar, but that was the last anyone offered to pay us. We couldn't oblige her because nothing was left.

She must have been in her mid-thirties with very fair skin that hadn't been ravaged by days on the road in the cold rain or sun. A small mole like a beauty mark was barely visible just above her lip on the left side. She pulled her jet-black hair neatly into a large twist that sat above her neck to meet the upturned collar of her black jacket. Prominent cheekbones complimented her deep-set eyes, like hazel craters. Looking into them was like entering a dark tunnel. I admired her long grey skirt and leather boots, wondering how she had happened to come to us. Her clothing indicated affluence, and I noticed no bags or luggage. She should have been in the safety of a Russian villa instead of roaming as a refugee.

With her came a distinguished-looking man, about her age. Clean-shaven except for slight moustache, he obviously hadn't been shunted through the countryside as we had been. Neither was overweight nor emaciated. They seemed inclined to stay a while to chat. Both were Russian physicians, well-bred, sophisticated, interested in everything. I romanticized Anna Karenina and Count Vronsky.

The four of us stood in the shambles of what used to be our vegetable garden. It had been a long time since Paul and I enjoyed intelligent conversation. Several hours must have passed as we chatted, but as I think back on our encounter, I can't recall our having asked them a single question about their experiences, nor did they offer any information. It was almost like having a surrealistic experience with their sudden appearance, then disappearance. We guessed they were returning to Russia. How were they faring in this region of Germans and Russians and Poles? How did they get here? Where were they staying? In short, and not because of any language barrier, they were the ones interested in us. Paul tried briefly to outline for them our personal history from the time of the invasion. They seemed quite well informed on current events of which we were completely ignorant.

"Did you know," she asked, "that Russia and Poland made a pact?"

"How can that be? There is no Poland left," protested Paul. "The country is full of Russians, and the Poles have scattered in all directions as they've been invaded from one side and another. The Polish government is in exile in London."

"Be that as it may," she continued. "The Russian authorities made their pact with Communist Polish officials who stayed at home and established an ersatz government. They call themselves the Polish Committee of National Liberation (PKWN). The two parties agreed that the northern part of East Prussia is to go to the Russians and Silesia will go to the Poles."

"But generations of Germans have lived in Silesia, establishing homes and businesses and farms," I exclaimed. "The Poles are a minority. Very few lived in the cities. Most were farmers."

The husband sympathized, "Though we are citizens of a country at war with your country--or recently so-- we understand your situation."

She continued, "In February Stalin, Churchill, and Roosevelt met in Yalta. The war was winding down, and they were already confronting post-war problems."

"Wasn't that premature?"

"They assumed the Allies would overcome Germany, but they would have to settle the Polish issue."

Paul interjected, "Well, yes. If the Russians pushed on to Berlin, they would be occupying Prussia and Poland. I'm sure the Poles wouldn't want to be governed by Russians any more than by Germans."

"The 'Big Three' were also asking each other what should be Poland's eastern and western borders.

I added, "We all know that Poland has had many borders throughout history. Certainly they will want their country to be as it was when Hitler invaded in 1939."

"It's a thorny problem. As we said, Russia recognized the provisional Lublin government of Poland early this year. The PKWN."

We were astonished. How could a small group of Poles speak for all of the population, especially in wartime, with the previous government in exile in London? Where were the Western powers when that agreement was made? How can it be valid?

Her husband continued, "I advise you to leave Silesia as quickly as possible before your sufferings are multiplied as the Poles continue returning."

Paul and I didn't know whether we should believe them or not. A history of mistrust had long pitted the Germans against their Russian adversaries. Now we were ready to trust the words of two strangers after a conversation of only an hour or so.

"We have Allied money from the West, but we need German Marks. We can give you 100 Marks worth of Allied money in exchange for 50 Reich marks."

I knew it was proper procedure for guests requesting a favor to make the giving of that favor advantageous to the person granting it, but their offer of two for one seemed overly generous. I wondered if we should trust them. Yet this couple was so convincing that Paul exchanged with them the sum the doctors needed. With fellow countrymen and in ordinary times building such trust would have taken years!

When the couple left, Paul and I looked at each other, stunned. What had we done with the little money we had saved? We had never seen Allied money before.

In addition, their disclosures greatly disturbed us. How could the Russians give away East Prussia? Surely the doctors were mistaken about the agreement. But if they weren't, we should probably leave right away.

10 TO 23 JUNE

Events of the following weeks served to corroborate the truth of the doctors' account. An endless and ever-changing procession came daily to the farmhouse. All were refugees, not knowing where to go and wandering, happy to be near the house for a night.

Some Germans had been relocated in Poland following the German invasion of 1939, after Poles had been killed or removed to labor concentration camps. The Germans no longer had the homes they left in the West, and they had taken several years to get established in Poland. With the war ending, advancing Russians had forced them to leave, just as the Russians had ousted us. Those resettled Germans were returning to claim their property. At the same time previously displaced Poles were returning to reclaim their territory, the very same land!

Other Germans, whose families had lived centuries in Silesia, like ours, and had been forced by the Russians to leave their homes, had the joy of returning quenched when they found only smoldering rafters and crumbling bricks, if anything recognizable remained. Those Prussian Germans no longer had the will to flee again. All was useless. Where would they go? This entire area was a garbage heap of humanity, people unwanted by the victors and by the defeated.

More and more Poles came through Augenfeld. Some had collected farm implements along the way. Others even had stray cattle left by the Russians; but being on foot, they had to abandon much of their loot. They wanted us Germans OUT of THEIR country, for they'd come to reclaim lands lost to Russia and formerly to Prussia by their ancestors. The newcomers settled in Augenfeld, whether they had been inhabitants there before or not. They were going to rebuild Poland. Some had been released from German slave labor camps and were filled with hatred. They didn't care that Paul and I were anti-fascists. They expelled German women and children from THEIR land, whether or not those women had worked with the Russians. Poles said they were still Germans and didn't belong in Poland.

The Soviet-controlled Polish military had a presence at the same time as did the occupying Russian military. Once the Soviets had forced the German army out of Polish-Prussian territory, the Polish Communist authorities joined the Soviets in expelling the civilian population or forcing them into labor camps. The Poles were "getting even," even if their wrath was directed at the non-military. For about ten days they repeatedly seized Paul for forced labor, but he skillfully played his relationship with the Russian military against the Poles and avoided being taken away. Ironically, we Germans found ourselves turning to the Russians for protection.

How were the Soviets going to repatriate so many people in their territorial jurisdiction? After the ceasefire, they no longer needed the large German slave force they had transported to Russia from eastern Silesia, so they sent some back home. Others were imprisoned indefinitely.

So flowing in all directions throughout Prussian Poland were people like us. In addition, Russia was exporting prisoners of war and recently imprisoned Polish and German forced laborers. From the opposite direction, internees from camps headed back to homes in the east from western Germany.

All joined the throng of the displaced. Most didn't know how they would travel long distances to get home or what they would find when they arrived. Some went east; some went west. Frau Kratz's husband could have been one of them.

Earlier, refugees like us found vacant farms and flats which had survived bombings and fires. That was before Prussians returned to their homes and forced out the "squatters," before the Poles returned to force out the Prussian Germans. We were lucky to have a connection with Frau Kratz and thus could stay on, though we thought we'd have to leave when her husband came back, if he ever did, and until Poles kicked all of us off the farm.

Open freight cars were loaded with booty of war, destined for Russia. Passengers lucky enough to obtain train transportation often rode on top of tools and industrial materials or squeezed among wooden doors, drawers, molding, window frames. No passengers fitted well into cars full of wires, cables, and military machinery and anything else metal. Then there were the loads of railroad ties and livestock. All to rebuild what the Germans had destroyed.

Fortunately, the butcher and a local farmer were amenable to bartering, so we managed to stay alive, though wretchedly. Little meat was available and cost dearly. Because that farmer lived some distance from the railroad, his crops had been spared. Businesses in Augenfeld that hadn't been destroyed remained open through the occupation and the exodus and the ingress. Wealthy Germans who had fled before the Russian invasion were returning to the towns they had left. They hadn't lost everything and wanted to trade cigarettes and pieces of clothing for potatoes or a little soup. A few even wanted us to take some of their family silver for food. I shook my head at the thought of their having taken such useless items with them into exile in the west and now carrying them back. Of course, they knew they would not get far with their precious heirlooms as they passed among thieving Russians and Poles, who also scavenged the roadsides for abandoned baggage and other treasures. Many items were too cumbersome to carry after wanderers abandoned travel by train in favor of tramping narrow roads.

Again and again I asked myself where they got the courage to travel. They could see no food was available in the countryside, so how could they expect to find any in the cities? Yet, with hope in their eyes the returning Germans repeated to themselves the magic word: "*Heimat*" (Homeland). They didn't yet realize that the cherished dreams in their hearts were a mirage. No longer did they have a "*Heimat*." Lttle did I know that I would become one of them.

The numbers increased from hundreds to thousands of refugees, or "displaced persons." Back and forth. Forth and back. A continuous flux. Thousands of people on the move. Berlin was a common destination for those who foresaw no future for themselves under either Russian or Polish rule. They heard that the Allies' treatment was more humane.

Getting by was easier if a former Nazi didn't look affluent. He simply professed his hatred of the Party and became a proud Communist. He rejoiced that the sickle would replace the swastika, knowing the advantages of having a new political identity.

24-29 JUNE | SUNDAY TO FRIDAY

Very little food remained for us, and we couldn't feed those who came begging. At the same time we feared harm from them if we didn't. Some refugees didn't make it as far as the farm but perished on the country roads. Others were pushed from trains. Paul heard about the abandoned bodies rotting in the sun.

He began to worry.

"My sugar and syrup are almost used up. If I have no more beer to barter, we are no better off than these paupers who pass through every day."

"You're right, Paul. There's no future for us here. In a way I feel responsible for Frau Kratz. I wish her daughter would come to care for her."

"We have no control over them. I wonder if I should go back to look for the Grammens. They should have been here by now. If we stay, we shall simply die of hunger."

"Like the refugees along the road."

"I am a bit hesitant about going back to Hilgendorf, for several reasons. I could be picked up by the Polish Communists; and even though the war is over, Russian authorities are probably still there, and I do not want to leave you and Fritzi alone, even for a day."

"At least the Russians that remain here know you, and you are of use to them as long as you can make beer."

"When I am of no use, they might send me off to a camp in Siberia. I heard from one of the refugees that some Germans were being detained up to ten years in the work camps at the same time as the ones already there were being released."

"But, Paul, where can we go? Masses are moving east. Masses are moving west. We've learned that Liegenbruch is designated part of new Poland."

"Yes, Hannah, I know you are right, but I have talked to many of our fellow countrymen as they pass through. Some don't believe the situation is desperate."

"Can you trust their assessment?"

"No, I cannot, but I am gaining a wider perspective every day. It seems Silesia has sorely suffered, at least here in the north, away from the mountains. In some places it appears we could possibly vegetate, but not live. Not live, Hannah."

"What do you propose?"

"Each day I have been pondering your question. One answer is to move back to my hometown, Hamburg. But I do not know if it has suffered during the war and to what extent."

"And how can we do that?"

"As yet, Hannah, I do not see clearly how to accomplish my plan. I spoke with Lüdtke. Do you remember him?"

"Yes, he was the village pharmacist. You found the yeast at his store after it was ruined."

"He is utterly dismayed over the situation, but he does not have the strength to undertake the burdens of migration."

"Will he be permitted to stay here in 'new-old' Poland?"

"I doubt it."

"You said the railroad worker didn't seem so distressed."

"No, he was in a good situation. He was alone, and an engineer from his brotherhood could help him."

I know Paul was thinking how difficult it would be had the rail man been burdened with a wife and child. I trusted he would devise a plan, for we had to leave.

Several times burglars broke into our farmhouse, but there was nothing to take. At least we thought there was nothing to take until we noticed robbers standing in our bedroom in the middle of the night. They took almost our last clothing! My blouse and skirt and sweater. Paul's pants and shirt. They were neatly folded in a pile in the corner where we'd put them before retiring.

Poor Paul! He found a tarpaulin the following morning, but I had no needle and thread to make any sort of primitive garment. He looked through the roads for something to wear. Refugees abandoned clothing, pots and pans, even blankets that became too cumbersome to continue carrying or impossible to take with them when a wagon broke down. Why couldn't the robbers have scavenged the roadside instead of invading our house? Outside, under some debris, Paul had stowed a pair of socks, his jacket, and an old pair of trousers. I hated living where every minute I had to consider whether or not to hide an ordinary object and why. We simply couldn't conceive such a degree of plundering. Yet each day it increased, especially at the railway station, where all the displaced congregated.

Paul shared his plan with me.

"I am considering our traveling on foot the 600K between here and Hamburg. My family may still be there. If we travel 20K a day, we would arrive in a month."

"What would we eat along the way?"

"Food will be a problem. We shall have to take every bit we can find here and eat very very sparingly."

During this conversation, a mother with five children arrived, asking for bread and food. She wore a bandana over her hair, but I could see it was brown, as were the dirty streaks across her face. A shabby dress, a torn sweater, shoes falling apart--all told her story.

I don't think she could have been more than 40. We had no need or desire to hear of her experiences. Everyone's were alike. She did say that she was German, heading west though she had no relatives in the Allied zones. She was simply propelled by fear of the enemy. Under normal circumstances her children would appear neglected, for they were as dirty and poorly dressed as the mother. We didn't ask about the father.

Both Paul and I were fully cognizant of our dire straits. Fritzi's hunger still gnawed on us. We looked at her smallest child, barely a year old, his belly distended and eyes hollow as those of a skeleton. He had a fever. How could we refuse? We decided to give Fritzi's gruel to the little fellow. His mother was thankful but disappointed that we couldn't completely fill all five hungry mouths. For months they had eaten only potatoes. But today! I spared one slice of bread! *Mein Gott!* To have endured all that suffering! It was a miracle they were still alive.

We put them on the parlor floor for the night. About 04:00 the mother awoke us to say the little fellow had died. She wasn't crying, for she probably had prepared for this loss and more to come. I suppose at some point she had become immune to tears. Paul got up to dig a grave. When he went to the tool shed, he discovered that the burgling Poles had stolen all the tools.

He went to the nearby churchyard to dig with an old tin can. It was hard work to prepare a grave in the dim light. He made it about 50 centimeters deep. Then he found an old paper carton so that he wouldn't have to put the naked child into the earth. However, when he came home to collect the infant, the body didn't fit. There was nothing larger, so he had to bend the little legs of the dead child. In so doing, he found the task too much. In spite of all his sorrow, he moaned loudly, "O God, isn't there enough suffering?"

I went outside to look around and found a little hand wagon behind the shed. A front wheel was missing, and the wood had been rotting for many years, but it could serve as a coffin. In spite of the rising sun, which promised a good day, my heart cried for the starving family and the mother who couldn't feed her children. So close to her loss had I been, but I still had my child. In the early light I gathered wild flowers and branches to decorate the makeshift coffin.

Paul carried the dead child outside and placed him in the new casket. Two small brothers dragged it to the cemetery behind the church, where so many unknown persons already slumbered, waiting for the last day. Wanting to say a few words of consolation, Paul asked, "Are you Protestant or Catholic?"

"*Gottglaubig*," she replied. (A believer in God) I really didn't want to be any kind of believer, but my husband said it would be better for me to have faith."

"And where is he now?"

"He fell in Russia. Killed in action."

I felt a tight knot in my throat as my husband recited the Lord's Prayer. Then all of us returned to the house. The woman thanked us for the shelter and said she had to keep heading westward toward Berlin. We could imagine the hardships she would be facing but were helpless to alleviate them for her. Berlin apparently was the "Promised Land," but it had suffered and probably had little to offer the influx.

"I cannot live here any longer," Paul complained. "I am wretched. Hannah, I am going back to Liegenbruch to see what is left for us there."

I felt somewhat safe staying at the farm since the threat of being raped by Russian soldiers had diminished. I didn't think the marauders would physically harm me, and Paul could make the round trip in a day. So he left and returned, left again another day and returned, left one final time and returned, convinced that our flat was completely uninhabitable, though he found some old clothing for us. Yet while he was imprisoned, I had gone back and found all just as we had left it. Probably refugees had trashed it as they passed through. I asked for no details, knowing that having lived in a shed had been acceptable to him, our flat must have been worse than I could imagine.

"Back there I ran into Krutchfeld from the physics department. He was convinced that everything will be better soon now that there is a cease fire."

"And you didn't believe him? How I'd love to go home again!"

"No, Hannah. Alspaugh, who lived down the street, took his family back. The four of them were poring over trash and digging where potatoes and onions might still remain in gardens. They are starving! They are starving!"

"Oh, Paul. Is there no hope?"

"They told me a local German government has been hastily established. I do not know how or who is in charge, but the Russians are playing the Germans against the Poles. All the complaints about property rights that the Russians do not want to bother with they shove aside or hand over to the new German administration."

"And how will those problems be solved?"

"Not by the Russians nor by the temporary government."

"Isn't there a Polish government set up there?"

"Not yet."

"So you don't want to go back."

"It is impossible. Madness. I was not deceived. No restoration will take place. In the few months since the Russians have occupied the city, not one business has reopened. Not one building has been restored. What happened to the plans for opening the schools again? The only thing happening is that the Russians are transporting to their motherland all the goods they can move."

"Then you're right. We must leave Silesia, or we'll go under."

"I saw Frau Grammen back there today. I told her that her mother had come back to the farm, and I tried to convince her to come here to the farm with us for a short while and then to leave Silesia with us."

"I'm so glad she's all right. Will all of them come?"

"No, she is afraid her husband will not find her, so she is staying there a while longer."

I left the decision and planning in Paul's hands. Once again he was feeling that he was not a pawn of fate but a free man capable of heading his family. First he consulted a Polish travel brochure, his mind open to all possibilities. Then he spent time at the train station to see the frequency of the trains and to determine how many kilometers we could travel by rail, not walking. The agents at the station couldn't see the reason for leaving. They weren't looking at the situation through the same dark glasses that Paul used.

He was convinced we should leave. I was convinced. Suddenly he could reach no decision. Using his typical scientific approach, he was gathering all data before proceeding. How many years had I put up with his vacillations? Why hadn't I married a carpenter or a plumber or any man who could make a decision and stick to it? He wasn't the man I thought I had married.

30 JUNE TO 4 JULY

At last and finally Paul made a decision.

"We must make all sacrifices to leave as soon as possible."

On June 26 the Poles had begun to return to Silesia en masse, in all haste driving away us Germans from the cities and villages of the region. The former isolated instances of their oppression were of the past.

Paul had learned while in Liegenbruck that some former inhabitants had returned to find their homes in shambles, but still livable if they made basic repairs. When all was restored to some order, in dashed Poles. Like children running late back into a school house upon hearing the bell, they hurried into empty houses or into those occupied by Germans. We were temporarily spared on the farm, perhaps because Paul had brewed beer for the Russians, who still maintained some control in the area. Nevertheless, we faced inevitable dispossession. Should we wait to be forcibly evicted or should we choose our own time to leave?

We watched our fellow countrymen, jamming all the country roads. Heavy-hearted, they carried with them the few belongings they still called their own. Should we join them or wait for the next group?

The situation was precarious for many reasons. Some people were too weak for the move. Half-starved, they started out only to collapse, fall, and die along the way. The exodus reached such proportions after three days that the Russians were unable to drive their trucks through the masses. The immediate solution was to forbid further evacuation. Safety anywhere was out of the question. We had to escape from not only the evacuees but also from the returnees.

The day following the edict to "stay put" we packed our little wagon and walked to the nearby train station. Rumors were flying in the village. Paul easily confirmed what the Russian doctors had told us, which was that in July the Soviet Union transferred to Poland territories east of the Oder-Neisse line. This transfer was not agreed upon by the Western powers, but the Soviets were in control of the territories. People were saying:

"The situation isn't hopeless."

"Germany won't be defeated."

"We're not leaving."

"It's only a temporary evacuation."

"Just let some Pole try to boot me out of my house."

"Silesia will remain German."

"The Poles will have to leave again."

When I tried to persuade Frau Kratz to leave with us, she argued, "No, I want to stay here in my house. I belong here. I'll be safe. I'll wait for my husband. If I left, he wouldn't know where to look for me."

I hoped Frau Grammen would soon decide to go to her mother and that the two could at least wait together. There should have been some way for her to leave a message. He knew the location of the farm in Augenfeid and might conclude that his wife and Rolf went to join her mother. On the other hand, maybe the mother should have left word for her husband and joined her daughter in Hilgendorf. The farm was in fair condition, ripe for a Polish take-over. God willing, the two women would not wait in vain for their husbands and suffer.

We remained three days at the station. No chance to get away. Either no trains, or they stopped on the tracks where no waiting passengers could board. If we moved to where the last train had stopped, the next train stopped somewhere else. Pure chicanery. Malicious teasing. But what recourse did we have?

Wearily we returned to the farm, exhausted from spent hope and missed sleep. How we needed rest!

Frau Kratz was happy to see us again, believing we had given up our plan to travel, but Paul was adamant. The farm was such a short distance from the station that he could keep constant vigil.

On July 4, just by accident, an unscheduled train stopped for a long time.

"Come, come! Hannah! Fritzi! Grab the wagon."

Our belongings remained packed, so we were prepared to dash at once. We ran immediately to the freight car. At last, our decision having been made, we were on our way. What relief to climb aboard, hoist the wagon, and sit down on the floor.

"Oh, Mutti, Vati, the train is moving," Fritzi exclaimed. Our family was together and headed by a decisive father. I let my muscles relax, resting an arm around Fritzi and my head against Paul's arm.

Other villages were in close proximity, and within about half an hour the train stopped. I assumed it was to take on more westbound passengers, but instead, all passengers had to get off.

We were not at the station proper, but nearby at a bare plot of ground. Paul learned that supposedly the journey would resume on the following day. We made ourselves as comfortable as possible, knowing that we'd have to spend the night in the open. In the open, yes! Open to the sky and open to robbers. The food we had planned to ration to ourselves over 30 days was gone, stolen by a band of young toughs who outnumbered us and were not stopped by any of the other refugees, who were fiercely guarding their own possessions.

Paul was certain we could not exist without food and would die along the way. Still fresh were his memories of the emigrants from the east who had died near Liegenbruch. He had helped bury too many women and children to subject us to such a fate.

"Hannah, we must return to the farm. We cannot continue without provisions."

Of course, I agreed, and we set off on foot with our little Bum Bum, much lighter now. Fritzi almost didn't finish the 20-K walk, which took the entire day. Our spirits were broken, our bodies were exhausted, and our hopes were completely crushed.

5 TO 19 JULY

"Hannah, I have given our predicament a great deal of thought," Paul began in his professorial tone early on the following day. "Our present situation is untenable. On one level, you and I and many other fellow countrymen do not deserve this treatment, not by the Russians, not by the Poles. We did not personally bring this upon ourselves, but our soldiers have made innocents suffer, and our enemies are seeking revenge, a very natural reaction. We have no recourse. We cannot use the train. The schedule is unreliable. We could be dumped anywhere and robbed again, as has just happened. It is just too dangerous for us."

Let him talk to himself. I was tired of listening to the same speech over and over.

"What do you propose? A hired car?" By this time I was ready to stay with Frau Kratz. I was tempted to give up, but when I considered how much more we might endure, I knew we had to try to get away.

"Hannah, there is no future for us here. It would be better to leave on our terms rather than to be forced out by the Poles."

I thought, "Ja, ja, ja. I've read that book before."

He continued. "We'll have to make our way on foot."

"Do you really think our little cart will last more than a few days?"

"No, no. Bum Bum won't go 600K. We need something else."

On the farm remained a broken-down carriage, which had made its journey from upper Silesia many years ago. Here was its final resting place. The front wheels had been stolen already, but Paul wanted only the rear axle with its wheels. He intended to fashion a large, sturdy wagon for us, but his task was not an easy one. In fact, it was much more difficult than he had envisioned because returning Poles and expropriating Russians had stripped the farm of all tools that he needed. Nevertheless, after 14 days of improvising he finished.

It was July, and Paul worried about the timing. Were we to be on our way by late July, we could be in Hamburg by late August, if all went well. But realistically, we had to consider a two-month trip, arriving in late September. We would have to spend nights in the open. The temperatures would be dropping. Again Paul was visited with memories of our recent experiences with robbers and his horror at burying the bodies of evacuees. Those visions were constantly on his mind. It seemed we were trapped: British and Americans were pressing from the south and the west, forcing evacuees east; Russians pressing from the east were forcing evacuees west. Displaced Germans and Poles scattered in all directions. The feeble and the crippled, unable to walk any further, crawled into ditches to die. Paul, knowing that in case of a breakdown or illness on the way, there would be more safety in numbers, tried to persuade the druggist to go with us. He had no success.

Opening a drugstore in Liegenbruch was his dream, and it persisted in spite of the Polish takeover. He had his own good reason because each day a new rumor gained strength that Silesia would remain German and the Poles would withdraw. Paul knew the man to be intelligent and weighed the druggist's words. Perhaps the druggist blindly hoped that all would return to the status quo. Paul wondered if he had declared himself a strong Communist to ally himself with the Russians. The two men hadn't discussed politics.

Since that horrible day when our soup and butter were taken by the Russian soldiers, I'd been trying to strengthen my faith, to seek goodness in our strife-ridden world. My husband and son were well, alive. I had my own strength. The Russians were no longer harassing us, though we felt their oppression. In spite of the fact that we didn't eat well, we had food again. We were relieved that some of Frau Kratz's friends had returned and resumed their former friendship with her. A spirit of generosity had developed. Each person shared whatever he had, no matter how little. The butcher especially tried to help everyone in such self-sacrificing ways as he could, though he was under the watchful eyes of the Russians and was in constant danger of being caught. The most he could do was to pass out bones and the innards of cattle. Paul foresaw the necessity of having a little fat on our journey, so he boiled bones and skimmed the fat from the cooled broth. After frying it, he preserved it in three small glasses. At the same time, he continued selling his beer for bread and flour.

Our new cart on the appropriated axle was much larger than the smaller one. We filled it with food and our only belongings, knowing that we would have to manage it by ourselves with no help from fellow travelers. The day was beautiful when we left, sunny and not too hot for travel. In four or five days we might reach Gölitz.

What we had not considered was that neither Paul nor I was strong enough to pull the wagon. Due to the weight distribution near the handle, a great deal of strength was needed to balance the load. In spite of our exertion, after 2K we had to give up. It was an impossible task, so we returned to the farm. There we transferred only the most necessary items to our old decrepit little hand wagon. Amazingly, the load weighed nearly 100K. Then we were off again to catch a train for a short distance and then to walk. Since we had gone only 20K on the first train toward Berlin, we decided to go in the opposite direction, to Dresden.

20 JULY | FRIDAY

With patience we waited all night at the station for a train going our direction. At 04:00 on 20 July we boarded a car, empty except for a Russian officer. He helped us climb aboard. Happy again, we were taking yet another first step. We thought that we would be delayed some time sitting on the tracks, but quite soon we heard the engine. I don't know how long we listened, but the train didn't move. Anxiety kept us awake, though we wanted to relax after having been awake all night. At last a noise, wheels moving, and we were off, but oh, so slowly. We could have walked faster, even pulling the cart. Our arrival time in Dresden was incalculable.

In a short while, we were stopped on a siding. The officer, less friendly now, searched us for weapons. He found none, but took from the cart all of Paul's clothing, the little there was, and all the immediately edible food. Our wagon now weighed considerably less. The officer tossed his loot to other Russian soldiers stationed along the tracks. Months before I had been pleased that the Russians universally liked children, and I was glad to have Fritzi with us.

A few soldiers climbed aboard, and soon Fritzi was crying loudly. Someone was taking his little jacket from him. It was the first time a Russian had mishandled him, not only taking his jacket but brutally shoving him into a corner.

"You speak not of this," warned the pasty-faced soldier.

"*Nein, nein,*" we chorused.

"You tell complaint, we kill you, and little one, too."

His warning wasn't necessary. Well we knew from too much experience the danger of speaking out. We were completely at the mercy of these vicious men. They remained on board.

Again the train started, moving more quickly. I pressed my head against the dirty window to see the countryside and was saddened to see a once thriving province completely devastated. How greedily the weeds had spread over the earth, wresting it from cultivation. Or bare charred land testified to recent fires. What a long time it would take to recapture the soil to provide food for millions of people. What maniacal delusions had afflicted the human spirit to bring about such destruction to Europe. How many years of privation might the continent face? Frequently we were shunted to a sidetrack so that freight cars loaded with heavy equipment could pass us on their journey to Mother Russia.

From their packs the soldiers took out what looked like small wrapped confections, but we soon figured out that they were bullion cubes. Evidently they didn't taste good, for one after another the men threw them from the train.

Approaching them, Paul ventured, "If you don't want them, give them to us, please."

The response was a shove from the officer, but two of the soldiers gave theirs to Paul, a total of seven. Both of us were thinking of using them as the base for some future soup. Such positive thoughts of a future meal somewhere temporarily cheered us until after traveling about 40K came the command:

"Everybody off!" I was surprised at how many people had been riding on top of the cars.

We knew the routine. We would wait there, spend the night, be robbed again, and possibly be sent back. Our wagon could be taken this time. No one tried to stop us as we moved away from the tracks, abandoning all plans to continue by rail.

About 16 K from where we were forced off lay Kohlwald. Though our hearts were heavier due to the stolen food and clothing, our cart was much lighter. I pulled the wagon while Paul shoved from behind with a long tree limb. Fritzi carried a milk can containing two liters of water. It was unfortunate we had to take along water, but almost all wells were either dirty or polluted.

Summer with its heat and humidity had arrived. I tried to disregard the strain on our exhausted bodies and to find the trip tolerable. I repressed my sighs and pursed my lips. Fritzi was so bravely trudging along with us that we didn't want to reinforce his unhappiness with our complaints.

"Oh, look ahead," pointed Paul, as we approached a forest. The promised shade of the trees sheltered marshy terrain, but we would have to cross a small river. Seeing no alternative to proceeding other than by a narrow abandoned train bridge, we faced an unexpected task: we had to unload the packed cart because its weight might cause the bridge to collapse.

Although the distance across was only 300 meters, it seemed much greater when we made four trips each, back and forth. Fritzi remained on the far side with our belongings, happy to sit down to rest. The empty Bum Bum itself was quite heavy, but Paul and I managed to carry it between us. He was completely worn out.

"I must have some rest, Hannah. I know you are very tired, too. Let us relax here for half an hour."

Little rest it was because thousands of mosquitos stirred from the grass to suck our fresh blood. Hurriedly we repacked the wagon. A short while before, when we got off the train with the soldiers, I gathered up the crumbs of a few cookies which they left behind. That was the only food we'd had since morning, and now the sun was low in the sky.

We needed to step up our pace. What a relief to see the roofs of Kohlwald in the distance, crowned by a church steeple to show us the center of the village. Our road out of the forest led us directly to a small Russian entry post that blocked our way. The guards would not let us pass into the town at that point. They directed us to another entry that we had to reach via a detour back through the woods, along a *waldweg* (forest path).

The town seemed a mirage. We were there, but we weren't. So back into the woods we went, keeping to the outer edge along the perimeter of the village. None too soon, the narrow path came out onto an unpaved road into a residential district. Deja vu! Another inspection post!

Before those Russians permitted us to proceed, they searched the hand wagon for weapons, meaning they wanted clothing. They took most of the clothes we had left, but thankfully they were being well fed and wanted none of our remaining food.

Once inside the village we sought an empty dwelling, and there were many. We entered the first one that seemed habitable. Paul and Fritzi immediately lay down on the floor. I made a seven-cube bullion soup for us to sip slowly to make it last, and I realized how fortunate we were to have it and a roof over our heads. I thought about the refugees who stripped our garden when we had more food to eat. I could no longer consider their acts as criminal as I did at the time. Stealing food can't be a crime when one would die without it.

21 JULY | SATURDAY MORNING

Although we had to sleep on a hard floor, my rest was one of the best I can remember. How long had it been since I'd known such tranquility? Fragments of pleasant dreams hovered in my consciousness like clouds passing softly across blue skies--my father's gently rubbing my back, running through fields trying to catch my older brother, my mother's patiently teaching me how to mend a torn seam. Where were my parents now? How were they faring during this endless storm?

Quickly I dismissed the pleasant memories and the concerns about which I could do nothing. I had immediate tasks. The first morning light encouraged me to get up. Both Fritzi and Paul had risen, folding their quilts and neatly fitting them into our cart. A piece and a half of bread would have to suffice for breakfast because I had to ration our food carefully if it was to last a minimum of a month. I knew we needed protein, but where would we get it? The skimpy breakfast didn't dampen our spirits that glorious day, for our hearts were filled with joy at the prospect of crossing the Neisse River by sunset. Rumors were that things were much better on the other side. No time could be lost dawdling.

The railway station was easy to spot with its twin brick towers. Hundreds of refugees crowded the platforms when we arrived. We questioned people here and there as we walked through the masses, ignorant of any procedure for getting transportation.

Everyone with whom we talked pretended to know everything about the trains and schedules, but no one knew anything. It was impossible to learn where the trains were going or how far or if they were running at all.

We wanted to go to Dresden. Others were headed for Görlitz. We watched trains coming and going, but due to the placement of the station, we could not ascertain accurately which direction was east, west, north, or south. The sun had risen high in the sky, erasing clues. Paul had an answer.

"I figure the trains loaded with industrial materials are rolling east, to Russia. The enemy is appropriating everything possible as quickly as possible. They've taken all the small scientific apparati and now are after large machines."

"Then if we can trust the dated timetable on the board, there are only two trains we can get," I offered.

"Stay here with Fritzi," he directed. "I'm going to try some judicious questioning."

I watched him approach a Russian lieutenant who had just stepped off a train that was waiting to go ahead. At once Paul dashed back for us to rush to the train before it left. It was going to Dresden. He would pay any price to get us aboard.

As we stepped up to enter a car, the Russians inside barred our way. Only in exchange for schnapps would they allow us passage. So we tried another car and another. We joined other refugees running thither and yon, back and forth, being refused everywhere and panicking that the train would pull out and leave them behind.

I felt the desperation of everyone. Then, with memories only too fresh, I recalled the value of clothing to our oppressors. I hadn't worn a visible skirt for weeks. Paul had cut my hair quite short to give me the appearance of a man, and I wore a pair of his trousers. He thought such attire would lessen the chances of my being raped since he wouldn't be able to protect me. Though he was tall, he was also 58 years old and very weak from loss of weight and beatings. If the Russians attacked him, he couldn't defend himself.

I approached a soldier standing on the steps of one of the cars. He was older than most of the others and stood stiff. His triangular face was like that of a wolf, with both cheeks slanting from his ears toward his chin. Likewise, his mouth didn't spread laterally beneath his nose but angled upward from lips that met in a point

I offered: "I give you pants. You put my boy and man on train with me?"

In spite of the heat, every day I wore a skirt beneath Paul's trousers to make them fit better.

"Nein, nein," he snarled, baring yellow fangs, as he began throwing from the train some parcels that had been loaded. Then presently, *"Ja, ja, geben,"* as he changed his mind.

I asked Fritzi to climb onto Bum Bum, and I quickly pulled off the pants. I must confess I was not sorry to surrender them because the heat was oppressive. Paul came to us, silencing his surprise at my change of habit. We began to climb the steps and to enter the car in front of the soldier.

"Nein, nein," he insisted, now pointing to Paul's and my shoes. Simultaneously, without consulting each other, we took them off and handed over our only sure means of travel. He let us pass through.

It seemed our anxiety about the train's immanent departure was erroneous because we sat on the tracks until 14:00. When the sound of the engine told us we'd finally be leaving, a horde of young boys, 10 to 15 years old, scampered aboard. Jabbering Polish, all were tanned and dirty from outdoor living. A few wore cutoff ragged pants, while all looked rather like wild animals with their long, stringy hair going in all directions. They squatted and climbed like monkeys in a cage, scattered through the car, then quietly settled down. A lad who sat across the aisle from me wore glasses with only one lens. I couldn't help noticing all the cuts on his bare legs and shoes much too big for his feet. Long fingers ended in dirty fingernails.

Up front stood a tall youth who surveyed the car and smiled at one of his band, showing some black, rotten teeth. He'd probably never had a dental appointment, poor kid. I was beginning to take pity on the horde when his smiled disappeared and I felt his powerful eyes on me. He lifted his head, almost thrusting forward a pointed nose. Suddenly his mouth turned down more in anger than in despair. He gave a hand signal, which was passed from boy to boy, as if they were confirming that they were on the train and getting away.

Paul was wary and mistrustful of them as they eyed luggage and bundles. Later he asked if I had noticed how muscular their arms and legs were. The very second that the train started forward, the band instantly came to life again. The leader threw from the train the bundles passed to him from the assembly line that had formed. Within seemingly seconds, when the train started to accelerate, he jumped to the ground, followed by boys holding in their arms all they could carry. We guessed that about 100 pieces of lighter luggage went overboard, the very last belongings of many of the refugees. We grieved with them, first at the shock and then at the loss. It was frightfully sad. Paul was stunned. He sat mute. He closed his eyes.

21 JULY | SATURDAY EVENING

Paul finally broke his long silence. "I hope the worst is over now."

"So do I. It's been so hard."

"The Russians have been savages, but they murdered very few, at least as far as we know."

"Ach, Paul. Was it humane to let so many people die of hunger? That's a sort of murder. And the rapes!"

"I would guess few women escaped their wrath. If I had been faced with witnessing that act, I believe I'd have died trying to save you."

"I've escaped so far. You were so wise to disguise me."

"Did our German soldiers do anything different?"

"I hope not, but you're probably right. Hitler started the war."

"Yes, we aggressors must assume the guilt," replied Paul, weighing his words, speaking slowly with his north German intonation.

"You say 'we,' Paul. But we are innocent, you and I and Fritzi all the others who didn't join the Party."

"Obviously not all Germans are guilty, and I would say that 80% of the Russians soldiers were amiable people."

"How can you say that? Have you forgotten how they treated you in prison and in the work camps?"

"Oh, I suffered from their cruelty, but when I sift through my memory, my contacts with them and under them, many were like children, impetuous and unreliable."

"Don't tell me you're going crazy now, all full of forgiveness?"

"It is just that I became aware of a different morality. They could feel compassion and at the same time not render assistance. I doubt they had a sense of community, as we have. I almost think they did not possess such a desire for revenge as a lust for plundering."

"Yes, an unquenchable lust. I didn't tell you what the Russian woman doctor told me. A famous Soviet journalist named Ilya Ehrenberg spoke of killing us Germans. He said if the soldiers kill one German, they should kill another because 'there's nothing funnier for the Russians than a pile of German corpses.' Can you imagine any educated person making such a statement? 'Nothing funnier!'"

Paul agreed: "He sounds insane, the epitome of evil. But I am sure famous Nazis voiced similar commands. We cannot dwell on such hatred. It simply engenders more. Let me tell you a pleasant story."

"Well, I'm listening."

"In one village I was told they opened a barrel of herring and brought out the liquor they had stolen to invite local Germans to a party--like a child's birthday celebration. They even drank from cups!"

"Ja, ja, ja, Paul. They pushed into Germany to have parties with us."

I was still so shaken by all the recent events that I couldn't understand his new attitude.

"Hannah, can you believe the Russians thought the Poles hated us and would take revenge?"

"They did. I saw little difference--oh, Paul. I don't know. Don't talk to me now about all these things. They are so abstract."

"Then we can be concrete. The Russians thought the German workers were capitalists. They were astounded at the low standard of living in our houses and considered their situation better at home."

"Well, one woman I talked to at the station told me that a Russian soldier didn't know what to do with a toilet stool. He stood on the seat and crouched. When she told him that wasn't the correct way, he said, *'Nix kulture.'*"

"He was probably a young fellow from the country where no such modern appliances exist. I'm sure there are people in Germany who might know no better than he."

"Ja, ja! That woman I spoke to had the cleverness of such a country person. Once, when she had to take a train from Leipzig, she had no ticket. Before the conductor came through, she put a large gunny sack on the floor in the luggage space and crawled into it, holding it shut at the top from the inside. She was a tiny person and could pass as baggage."

"I'm sure the war has forced people to come up with many creative solutions. Those are all individual cases. For the most part, if people are accustomed to subvert their wills to authoritarian control, they will be easy prey to party organizers. Individual actions like hers were buried."

"Well, Paul, there were people like us who didn't follow Hitler. There were people who left Germany."

"True, Hannah. Do not remind me. Let us keep in mind that we Germans have always been a people who respect titles like 'professor' and uniforms."

"And flags!"

In retrospect I half wished or more that Paul had not been so circumspect in deciding to stay behind. I didn't want to be critical of his decision, but couldn't we have been saved all our suffering by having left?

As if reading my mind, he added: "Oh, we stayed and did not join the party, but do not tell me we did not feel oppressed. Do you know what kept me going when I was near death? It was not only what I felt for my family but what I wanted for myself."

"You've never told me."

"I want freedom--freedom in my thoughts and in my words, freedom in my *Weltanschauung* (view of the world), freedom in my profession, freedom for us to form a democratic government, freedom in how I conduct my life. I won't miss what possessions have been taken from us. I miss the freedom the Nazis took from me."

"Yes, they were criminals in many ways."

"They took my intellectual energy. They robbed me of my spirit. One man took advantage of our weakened economy and recognized the sick spirit of our people. How blind they were to dumbly climb aboard his feeble lifeboat. The best German people had to stand aside or perish in the KZ (concentration camps). The majority was barely aware of the enormity of the Nazi atrocities."

I had never heard him talk in this vein and to this length. What he was articulating about our people I knew, but he hadn't revealed the depth of his invisible wounds.

About that time the train was slowing and stopped in Wehrkirch for all to get off. Already it was 16:00, and we knew we would be delayed until the next day at the earliest. Again thousands were lying on the ground near the tracks. We knew what was ahead-- more robbing and rape.

"*Schnell*! Hannah, Fritzi, this way."

Paul hurried away from the station, pulling our hand wagon by himself at first. His mental unburdening seemed to have given him physical strength. One never would have thought him a professor by his present looks. He was unshaven, had matted hair and wore a mechanic's suit with torn short pants. The suit was the result of a barter in exchange for three kilograms of flour and some other food. I looked no better in my wrinkled and soiled skirt, though I was more comfortable not wearing Paul's trousers. Both of us were shoeless. My hair was only a bit longer than Paul's. Fritzi had a shirt, pants, and shoes and probably wasn't missing his stolen jacket in the warmth of mid-July. I refused to think of our future in such dire poverty.

22 JULY | SUNDAY

We hurried away from the tracks to get out of sight and walked for about two hours before finding a barn which promised shelter. Other refugees had the same idea as ours, and we formed a small procession in the dust, dirt, and heat.

With us was a young woman of 28 with her five-year-old daughter and eight-year-old son. Because she had no male protection, she wanted to continue traveling with us. I smile recalling her naiveté at expecting a single aging man capable of protecting two women and three children. She wanted to know about our experiences and shocked us with her own:

"It was early in the evening--we had finished *Abendessen* [evening meal]--when Polish soldiers barged through the door and demanded we leave at once. They had some kind of rubber clubs and hit me because I didn't move fast enough, but they told me I had only ten minutes to get what I wanted to take. I really wasn't surprised that they came because I had heard that in neighboring villages the people had been forced out. I didn't need a lot of time to gather up belongings because the Russians had already taken so much. Several men raped me in front of my children. The soldiers then took my husband's clothes as a souvenir and said 'to remember you.'

"They told me the house was going to be given to Poles. We didn't expect them in our village so soon and that they would expel us and shove us through the streets like cattle. It was getting dark, and I had my two children with me. We walked several hours to a filthy camp and had to stay there about a month. There weren't enough sheds at the camp to house hundreds people in cramped quarters. I asked if I could sleep outside with my children, but one of the guards hit me and said we would try to run away."

"Where did they think you would go?"

"I didn't know where we were. They gave us only bread and water for the first few days, hoping some of us would die. After priests heard about the camp, some came with food, and that was almost worse than having no food because everyone fought for a scrap. And there I was with two children to feed. I couldn't fight the taller people, and no one wanted to share. Sometimes the guards wouldn't even let priests in when a person was dying.

"At last they loaded us onto cattle trucks. Some of the people were quite old. Typhus and cholera were spreading like fire on dry leaves. It didn't matter to our captors. They threw us all together, even the crippled ones. Some of the men, older than regular soldiers, were taken away to a labor camp. You should have heard their wives and children crying. They probably would never see their fathers and husbands again.

"The trucks climbed a steep hill. Of course, I couldn't see where I was, but when I got out, I found myself at a castle, but not to live like a queen but to die in the dungeon. All of us were dumped into a damp basement, filled with excrement and rags. At first we didn't see the rats, but at night we could feel them crawling on us. Some sisters brought us hot soup every day. The little bread and cheese that I took from home when we left had been eaten long before. It didn't matter because it would have been taken when the soldiers made all of us go outside to be searched. While that was going on, some of the soldiers went into the cells to ransack our belongings. Lots of people complained that their food was gone, along with some jewelry and money. Every day the guards passed by, hitting us with their rifle butts, just for fun. If anyone had died overnight, they made us haul the body out to the yard. I don't want to guess what they did with it.

"I'm not sure how long we were in that cold place before we were again packed into trucks and taken to a rail station somewhere. The trains that came were full of people like us. We had to wait all night and until noon the next day before they came back to pile about 75 of us into one truck."

"Had you any idea of where they wanted to take you?," Paul asked.

"We thought they would take us to the border, and they did, but the Russians had closed the border, so the trucks turned around and took us back, but not to the castle. Instead they stopped on a narrow road and told us all to get out. My children were so exhausted that they could hardly walk, but it was good to be able to move and to be away from the soldiers. We went from farm house to farm house, begging food. Now it was Poles we were begging from because they had houses that had belonged to Germans. At first they gave us some food, but there were so many people passing through that they even stopped answering the door. Lots asked us to pay for any food that they gave us. If we didn't have money, and who did because we had been robbed, they wanted clothing or shoes and boots. If a person had decent shoes, not all worn down and torn, they were sacrificed for food and worn-out shoes. You can imagine that usually the shoes didn't fit and we ended up with sore feet and blisters."

After her long narrative, we learned she wasn't going in our direction. Paul advised her to continue on foot. Without a doubt, further travel by rail, if it was even possible, was fraught with too much danger. She was about 60 K from her destination, and we wished her well as they parted from us at the next crossroad.

A long, tiring walk lay ahead for us. At least we hadn't been molested once, but our hunger was extreme. Each day our self-imposed allotment was no more than a quarter kilograms of flour for three people.

For those who didn't witness the exodus, it must have been impossible to visualize roads crowded with so many thousands of people on the move. As I walked along, I thought about my underclothes. At home I changed them daily or every two days at the most. Now I had worn the same ones--dirty, with holes, smelling of perspiration--for several months. They became my second skin. I became a disgrace to myself, a disgusting hausfrau, but that self was another woman. Now I was Hannah the refugee.

23 JULY | MONDAY

It was a godsend that we were able to keep our cart, for along the way Fritzi collapsed. As Paul lifted him, I felt such angst. He was dying. If only we could get to some place to rest for a while. My worry was doubled when Paul's strength suddenly disappeared. In Baufal he threw himself onto the ground, falling into a deep sleep. I myself could hardly put one foot in front of the other.

What was I to do? Both my son and my husband needed rest and nourishment. If I were to increase our daily ration, we might starve before reaching Hamburg. And then what? We didn't know if Paul's parents were still there. Should I, too, stretch out my weary bones on the ground beside them? Unthinkable! We could be robbed and then surely we would die of starvation.

Again I found myself completely alone with no one to rely upon. Previously, when Paul had been taken away, at least I had Fritzi for company. Now I might lose both of them. Fortunately it was noon, so most of the evacuees were not ready to stop for the night. I spotted the steeple of a school house not far off.

"Paul, Paul, get up, get up! At first gently and then more forcefully I shook his shoulders. You must help me get Fritzi to that building over there!"

He slowly got onto his feet, barely able to stand without quivering, and sloughed in the direction I indicated. It seemed suicidal for me to think of pulling the Bum Bum, which now contained Fritzi in addition to our few remaining goods. I had no choice, and somehow from somewhere came a surge of strength to my arms. I could slowly pull the load. Perhaps there was an almighty being looking after us.

Once inside the abandoned building, I had to take charge. "Paul, you must stay awake! Do you understand? You must guard our cart. You can't fall asleep again. Do you understand? You stay here with Fritzi. Stay awake and guard the cart. I'm going out to find us something to eat."

He gave me a dazed look; his vacant eyes didn't indicate that a word I had said had penetrated his consciousness.

I had no choice other than to leave the two of them there. My legs felt weak as noodles as I set forth on my mission.

I continued on the road which seemed to be the main street through the town, always looking back at the steeple of the school to keep aware of my location. I would have to find my way back. I explored the side streets. From office to office I scurried, like a mouse seeking crumbs. Because of the hordes of *Flüchtlinge* (refugees) passing through the town, there were signs showing us many stations set up for assistance. If I didn't find something, both Paul and Fritzi would be dead in a few days at the most.

There was no time to consider my own weakened condition. After a few hours of desperate searching, I went into a small office away from the mainstream of searchers. My story of starvation met compassionate ears and voila! The man who took time to listen went into another room and came back with a whole loaf of fresh bread. A whole loaf! And it was fresh. The first fresh bread in five and a half months!

I flew back to the schoolhouse. I don't know how my previously wobbly legs carried me with such speed. As I expected, Paul and Fritzi were asleep. Luckily, they were still alone and the cart was intact.

"Smell, smell!" I exhorted, putting the bread beneath Paul's nose as if reviving him with smelling salts. He didn't stir. Then I shook him and let him sniff the bread. He thought he was dreaming. It took extreme effort to rouse him and then to convince him. I think that deprivation affected his brain.

The Russians had permitted us to keep one of the three jars of preserved fat. I had to use it now. Fritzi was awake and joined us in falling upon the bread. We were like wild animals devouring fresh prey. We couldn't control ourselves. I think we gobbled up half the loaf in our first bites. At once the world was a different place.

"Oh, Hannah, Hannah! How blessed I am to have you for a wife. You are so brave! So unselfish. You have never complained."

"I do what has to be done."

"Many a time I thought about the men who sent their wives into Central Germany, to safety. How I reprimanded myself for selfishly keeping you and Fritzi with me, for not taking all three of us away. Ach, so much would I have spared you!"

"We can't look back now, Paul. You had no idea how the war would end. We couldn't foresee the Russian invasion, the return of the Poles."

"Here we sit in Baufal. We have only the clothes on our backs. We do not even have shoes. We are starving. This is the very brink of annihilation."

"No, Paul. We're still alive and together and we have fresh bread."

"The scoundrels responsible for all this misery escaped, were they major or minor party officials. How I detest even hearing the word 'Nazi.'"

"Then don't say it."

"It is true. They are safe with most of their belongings, undoubtedly denying their deeds and affiliation. Well, we must not waste energy now feeling sorry for ourselves or blaming them. We need to plan ahead."

Yes, the same old words, "plan ahead." How many times had I heard them. At that moment I wished he would go back to sleep.

I, too, was "planning ahead." I told Paul the man who was in charge of bread commented that Hamburg is quite far.

"There's a possibility of getting a train to Dresden if we can get to Domitz. It's only about 10K away."

"I think we can do it now. We've come this far."

So we three settled down for the night, even though it would be light for many more hours. When a body is so weary, the hour of day and the position of the sun are of little importance. My feet burned and stung from cuts caused by walking barefoot. Lying down to sleep didn't alleviate the pain. All of us *Flüctlinge* had been robbed so many times that every person on the road had a pack light enough to carry. No longer could one find along the way a dry blanket, a warm jacket, or shoes.

Today, so far from those days, I find it nearly impossible to understand how much nourishment that loaf of bread provided. Our spirits perked up at the same time as did our bodies. The next morning we cheerfully continued our journey.

24 TO 26 JULY
TUESDAY TO THURSDAY

Along the way we lost time when the cart broke down and required repairs, but by 17:ll we had reached the railroad station where a freight car waited. We crawled in and thanked the Lord we'd had a decent sleep the night before. How many years of my life had I gone from day to day, never appreciating having had a good bed or a good rest. Such little things in life now were "gifts." There wasn't even space to sit down in the car, let alone lie down, so we stood. Even though the train pulled out shortly, it soon stopped for the night and didn't move again until dawn. At least we could stay aboard, and in the early morning I couldn't believe we were finally in Dresden-Neustadt. We were actually in Dresden! Out of Silesia! Away from the Russians! Away from the Poles! And Paul had a sister in this city!

"I want to find Grete and her family if they are still here. They may have been victims of the terrible air raid on 13 February."

"What? I didn't know about that. We know so little of what's happening anywhere."

"I talked to a rather knowledgeable man at the railroad station while we were waiting for this train. He tried to discourage me from coming, insisting that very little remained of this beautiful city. I felt we had no choice after our experiences in trying to go to Berlin."

As I looked at Paul, I could read concern on his face as he was confronting our new problem. Of course, he'd been worrying about his sister.

""You must tell me more. Don't try to protect me because we're here now."

"The fellow told me that the old sector was completely obliterated with the first heavy British bombing. Then a second wave of planes released their cargoes further south.

The Americans came the following day for rail yards and houses. The people are completely demoralized."

"Then the Frauenkirke church must have been damaged."

"I suppose the cathedral fell with the rest of the destruction in the old town."

"*Ach, mein Gott*! Your sister and her family might be dead. They lived close to that sector."

"That remains to be discovered."

"Oh, Paul. Dresden was a jewel. Baroque churches lured tourists from the whole world. They were centuries old. And the beautiful Stadtschloss! [City Palace]. I hope it was spared."

"He said many of Dresden's factories had been converted for making military equipment and that a good many German troops could always be found here."

"This will be a difficult visit."

"According to him, the city burned for seven days, and the firestorms created winds as strong as hurricanes."

"I can't even imagine such destruction. I do hope your sister's family is all right and that we can stay with them a short while."

"Yes, Hannah, so let us not linger here at the station any longer."

After we'd walked a short distance, Paul announced:
"I am first going to knock on a few doors to find a safe place to leave you and Fritzi with the wagon. I cannot expect you to traipse around the ruins with me, and you two need some rest after our standup night."

It took little persuasion for him to convince me that he was strong enough to look for shelter, and he wasn't gone long at all. After my Herculean exertions of the previous day, I was a basket case.

"Come, Hannah, Fritzi. I found down the street here two friendly women who say they can make space for us and for our cart."

Hurriedly we followed him as he grabbed Bum Bum and started off to the house. A young man opened the door at once. He was about 20 and obviously a factory worker. His hands were stained as if from dark oils, and his blue overalls also revealed oil streaks. He went immediately to Fritzi, and fear gripped me. But it was for naught because he thrust his own breakfast bread and butter into Fritzi's hands and then disappeared as quickly as he had appeared. He didn't even stay long enough for us to thank him.

Fritzi stood white as a corpse, the bread in his hand. He didn't know what to do, what to say. Paul was aghast, frozen by a storm of emotions. This was real! Someone had actually given something instead of taking it away. Incredible!

"Now, Hannah. I am going off. I do not want to lose any time in finding my sister's house."

The kind women found a quiet room for Fritzi and me. I was so exhausted that I hardly looked at the woman and wouldn't recognize her were I to see her again. The sisters knew how tired we were and wasted no time with conversation. Paul had apprised them of our recent experience and fatigue. Fritzi and I put down our bedding and quickly fell asleep. Until now, with the spontaneous gesture of kindness to Fritzi, I had held up, propped by psychic energy from above. At last I could let down, dissolve for a while.

When Paul returned, after being gone a considerable time, his expression puzzled me.

"I started across Augustus Bridge and hardly reached the other side before I fully realized the extent to which Dresden had been razed, demolished. I walked 5K and saw not a single house--only a streetcar line running between ruins. People were running here and there, obviously busy with some tasks, but what was there to do? Debris was all I could see. Charred wood was all I could smell. If a second floor remained in a building, the stairs to reach it were gone, leaving gaping holes in a ceiling."

"What of your sister's house?"

"Gone. I stood in front of the ruins, overcome by an unspeakable depression. I was suddenly struck by the horror she must have suffered. The thoughts coursing through my mind are making me dizzy.

"I was just turning to leave Grete's house when my eyes fell on a few chalked words: 'Krugs now on Strehlener Street.' I gave a shout: 'They are alive!'"

"Probably they're as destitute as we are."

"I was so full of joy and inquired of the first person I encountered how to find the street. I hoped it was not far because you know how tired I am--and barefoot. With so much rubble underfoot everywhere, I had to watch every single step."

"Did you find them?"

"Oh, yes. They are living in a house with many other families who were bombed out, and they don't know how long they can stay there or where to go. Grete said many refugees had arrived in Dresden before the bombing and were victims. Bodies had to be burned to avoid typhoid. We could not talk long because I was so weary and wanted to get back here."

"You must have been relieved, even if there's no room for us to stay with them."

"The two women here say that we can stay for a few days' rest before we go on."

"Such kindness. I don't know how to take it after all we've been through."

"Right now I am just heartily grateful and must get some sleep."

The following day, relatively refreshed, we told the two women that we would be away for a few hours to see Grete. Although months had gone by since the February bombings, the stench of burnt timbers was overwhelming. I had already seen farm buildings destroyed by advancing Russians, but never could I have prepared myself for such mass-scale destruction. Walls stood around hollow innards, their windows gone and reminding me of photos of the Coliseum in Rome. Paul was lucky to find the street where his sister was because some areas were so piled with wreckage that streets were impassible. We tripped with our bare feet over rubble everywhere. A wind had arisen on that warm day, but instead of welcoming it, we covered our faces for protection from the ashes it stirred up. They invaded our nostrils and eyes, even clinging to my eyelashes. Our ragged clothing looked even more shabby under the white film. To keep the soot out of our mouths and throats, we refrained from talking.

Once reunited with Grete, we didn't stay long with her and her children. They didn't have to tell us of the horrors they suffered, the fear for their lives. Neither she nor Paul could assure the other of where to find each other in the future. Our plans to use their parent's home in Hamburg for refuge or as a communication station were out of the question. Grete had received notice that both their mother and their father had been killed in the bombing of Hamburg.

My heart ached for Paul. Besides having withstood invasion, expulsion, and incarceration, he now had the sorrow of seeing the suffering of his sister and of losing his parents.

The walk back to our shelter with the sisters was over broken cement and glass. The chance to rest a few days to help our bodies and spirits recover was truly welcome. The sisters' family hadn't any more food than we, so we each ate only our own. In our calculations for what food we'd need to get to Hamburg, we hadn't counted on extra days of travel.

27 TO 29 JULY
FRIDAY TO SUNDAY

We left Dresden by train. Again Russian soldiers were aboard, much to our surprise. We feared what they might do, so we left the train at our first chance, crossing the Mulde River at night and resting in fields during the day. Another train took us through Leipzig to Halle. After that we saw no more Russians.

Even though people had ration cards, no food was available in Halle, and travel out of town was impossible due to the overwhelming crowds at the station, all waiting to go to major cities. We had to keep going, so the practical solution was to catch a local train to Eisleben, which we found had been spared the devastation of Dresden.

I was beginning to wonder how much longer we could subject our child to such taxing exertion. Unable to rest, unable to wash, unable to change clothes, unable to eat enough, we barely kept alive from one day to the next, traveling constantly. Our fears propelled us, previously fear of the Russians and now fear of an outbreak of typhoid fever. It seemed heartless to go on, but there was no stopping. After we had stepped from the train and started down the street in Eisleben, Fritzi collapsed for the second time.

"Leave your boy with me while you find a place to sleep," urged a woman walking by. "Then you can get him again."

We were conflicted. Could we trust her? Was she a good Samaritan? Could others be concerned for our wellbeing? Miseries of their own had hardened most people up to now. Yet there were the two kind women who sheltered us in Dresden. We had no choice. Paul again put Fritzi on Bum Bum, and we went with the woman to her house, which fortunately was very close to the station.

"Mutti, where are we?" he questioned as he was reviving.

Paul was heartened to see Fritzi's recovery and knew he had to find a place for the three of us. I stayed with the woman and Fritzi, lying next to him on the floor of the woman's parlor with the warm sun pouring in upon us.

"You're with me, son," I reassured him. "We're going to rest here for a while. Vati is finding a place for us to stay. Let's go to sleep now."

30 JULY TO 1 AUGUST

Our luck soared. Paul had found a royal welcome at the home of a widowed physician's wife, Frau Bauer. He put Fritzi on the cart to prevent his collapsing again, and we hurried to her house.

She greeted us warmly at the door.

"Come in, Frau Merkel. And this must be Fritzi. I heard all about you."

We entered a well-appointed house and were shown into a parlor to sit down. Frau Bauer was of medium height and weight, dressed in a neat skirt and ironed striped blouse. As was the style of most women, she twisted her gray hair into a bun. It shone silver in the sunlight filtering through unbroken windows. The room was furnished with a flowered carpet, crocheted antimacassars on chair arms and backs, a heavy mahogany buffet against one wall, a lamp table with a marble top--so much I couldn't take it all in. Yet, we didn't belong in that room as we were. I protested.

"Oh, no! We are too dirty to sit down on your beautiful furniture."

She acquiesced.

"I understand how you feel. Perhaps you would enjoy a bath, and my housemaid, Tillie, will wash your clothes for you."

"I can think of nothing in the world I would like more."

"I see you're in need of clothing, too. Let me get some for you."

"Oh, no, thank you. I can't accept such a sacrifice when you surely need them. I know they can't be replaced very soon."

"No, no. My pleasure will be so great if you say 'yes.'"

I couldn't refuse, and the beatific smile on her face was an additional reward. I vowed that for the rest of my life I would always try to show generosity to equal hers.

"I have beds for you, too. Follow me."

We were speechless as she led us upstairs to a bedroom and adjacent bathroom. Tillie soon appeared with fresh towels and a small piece of soap.

"Frau Bauer and I want you to accept these poor pieces of underwear. They're not new, but they're clean and in good condition."

She had coarser features than Frau Bauer, and her muscular arms showed that she had used them for more arduous tasks than washing clothes and carrying towels. I felt it wasn't my business to engage her in any conversation about herself. Besides, I was so tired that washing myself and helping Paul give Fritzi a bath was all that I could manage. I shall remember the rest of my life the luxury of removing my putrid clothing, the feel of clean warm water and soap on my body, the sight of dirt washing away, drying my body with a clean towel, and putting on clean garments.

When I looked into their clear eyes, I thought that those two women were saints, just as Frau Kreidler had been for Paul months ago. They even found a few pieces of underwear for Paul.

It was glorious to lie down on a real bed. I could hardly remember the comfort of a mattress, sheets, and a plump feather pillow.

When we awoke the next day, our clothes were clean and dry, piled outside our door. We intended to get an early start, but the skies were dark with heavy rain falling. Jove hurled thunderbolts and lightning to earth.

"Oh, you can't leave yet!" Frau Bauer exclaimed. "You need at least another day and night to rest after all you've endured. And I want to prepare a meal for you."

Had I heard correctly: she wanted to prepare a meal for us? Surely I was hallucinating. I'm sure before that invitation both Paul and I were wondering how we could reduce our daily flour allotment to extend our food yet another day. We still intended to go to Hamburg, even though we knew we wouldn't find his parents and we would find considerable damage there. It was near midday, the time we usually ate our "big" meal while sitting on the ground somewhere. Today Frau Bauer ushered us into her dining room. Was I dreaming? Was this a moving-picture set? A white cloth covered the table. Knives and forks lay beside plates. Her centerpiece consisted of greens from her yard.

"I didn't have time to plant flowers," she apologized.

I was speechless when she served young peas and carrots, and when I looked at Paul, tears were running down his cheeks. This stopover of luxury and rest were vital for us. After we ate, the sun came out, and Paul left to explore the town. He hoped to find some shoes for us. Unfortunately, Frau Bauer's feet were smaller than mine, just as her husband's were much smaller than Paul's.

Though Paul was unsuccessful in his shopping expedition, he didn't seem unhappy when he returned.

"Hannah, you will be amazed at what I have to disclose. I inquired in town at the agency dealing with refugees and made arrangements for us to go to the border of this zone in an ambulance. We leave tomorrow morning."

"I can't believe it! Deliverance has really come!"

That night excitement kept me awake for a long time, and we were up early to thank our hostesses and to depart.

2 TO 7 AUGUST
THURSDAY TO TUESDAY

In a village only 9 K across the border I had a cousin whom I hadn't seen nor had contact with for years All I knew of her was that she had married. I doubt that she had heard anything about me since I was in my early teens. For all I knew, she wouldn't be living in the area any more, but it was worth taking a chance to search. The ambulance dropped us at the line, and we walked to the area where I thought she last lived. We stopped at several farms to inquire about her whereabouts and for directions. Luckily the family had always referred to Hilda's husband by his last name, Mitteldorf, so our task was made fairly easy. I'm glad we got an early start in the morning because it was a hot day. Even though we didn't have a lot in our cart any more, anything can be a burden when the heat is oppressive.

Cousin Hilda was about my age. Her mother and my mother were sisters, raised on the same farm. Mother said her sister was always rebellious, would accept little or no discipline from their parents. She hated farm work and one day ran away with an itinerant day worker who happened by at harvest time and stayed a few weeks. Only several years later did she let her parents know she had married and settled further south.

There the couple raised a son and a daughter. When I was a teenager, my aunt took her children north to meet us relatives. By that time my grandmother was old and my grandfather had been dead for five years. Rigorous toil on the soil had worn out his body and worn down hers.

Hilda and I had little in common. I was a serious student and a reader. She preferred frivolity. But we did get along. Some twenty years had now passed by.

I recognized the woman who came to the door by a large mass of blonde curls, which she wore cut short, unlike most women. She was stout, even overweight, showing she hadn't been deprived during the war.

"Guten tag, cousin Hilda. I'm your cousin Hannah Vogelsang."

"Ach, mein Gott! I haven't seen you since we were young, and you didn't want to have fun. We were just children then."

"I have my own child now. This is Fritzi. He's eight, and this is my husband, Paul."

Admittedly, we were not such a sorry sight as we would have been, thanks to the generosity of Frau Bauer. Hilda didn't immediately invite us inside, but she seemed to have little choice.

"Do come in. All of you."

She wore a patterned cotton dress, cotton stockings, sensible shoes. Her blue eyes were cold, and her voice lacked warmth. We three followed her into the kitchen, where we sat on stiff wooden chairs.

"What are you doing here?" she queried, her mouth firm.

Paul briefly explained our experiences. Then I asked about her family.

Hilda's brother, as mine, had been killed in the previous war. Her two sons had been in the German army, both having fought in France. One, Wolfgang, had come back home. She didn't know where the other one was.

At that moment a tall, athletic-looking man came into the house with a basket of carrots and tomatoes. The sight revived old memories of our own previous gardens.

"This is my husband, Horst Mitteldorf."

He was twice the size of Paul, who had lost an enormous amount of weight. Ruddy cheeks gave evidence of prime health, and he extended a strong arm to shake hands. He was much younger than Paul, and I wondered how he had avoided conscription. Or had he been a Nazi official and was now posing as a farmer? I dared not ask. At any rate, someone had been able to maintain their home and garden. All appeared untouched by the war.

"Hilda, we're trying to make our way to Hamburg, but we desperately need shelter for a while. As you can see, Fritzi's clothing hangs on him as on an empty hanger."

Then in a whisper, I told her, "Paul and I fear that after all we've endured he may not be ours much longer."

"Oh, I see. You are Flüctlinge."

She hissed the word as if it were a hot coal in her mouth.

More honestly she might have said, "You are "undesirables." "Well, yes," she hesitated. "I guess we could give you a little help."

At the same time she looked apologetically at her husband and shrugged her shoulders.

Fritzi had slumped on the table, his head in his hands.

"Is there somewhere here where we may rest now? We've walked from the border and are quite tired."

"I suppose I can give you Heinrick's room, though he may come home any day. It has only one bed, so you'll have to use the floor."

"We've slept on the floor and on the ground, and even tried it standing up. Thank you, Hilda."

It was very late afternoon when we went upstairs in the farm house to sleep. Paul and Fritzi drifted off at once. Though I had lost about 9 kilograms and was weak, relaxing was difficult for me.

I soon smelled meat cooking, but we weren't invited to partake of the evening meal. Usually the main meal is cooked at noon, but I didn't know what was the family custom here. The following two days, Hilda gave us bread with chicken fat at noon and in the evening. We also had some carrots, tomatoes, and potatoes with each meal and some ersatz coffee in the morning. Fritzi hadn't eaten for three days and couldn't force a bite. His condition didn't arouse any sympathy in our hosts, who probably thought he was being picky. The next day he slowly recovered a desire for food and regained a little strength.

Oh, yes. Those farmers had chickens and eggs and curd cheese, but that food was not for us undesirable exiles. Hilda, Horst, and Wolfgang ate their meals apart from us, and always earlier. We kept mostly to our room with Fritzi, though Paul became restless and took short walks.

Here away from the Russians and Poles, I could relax and hope. We had no idea of where we would live or on what. Paul walked to the nearest town to look for authorities to help him cash an insurance policy. He learned he could execute his plan, but the devaluation of our currency had reduced the policy's value to only 1,000 Reich marks. That sum would not last long.

Wolfgang briefly nodded to us when we were near him. Neither Hilda nor Horst invited us to sit with them in the parlor or on the open porch after eating. Here were my cousin and her family closing rank against us exiles. I was later to learn that most refugees in Germany were experiencing the same antagonism. People like us weren't welcome anywhere. Blood ties with my cousin were like frayed string when we needed rope. Her family wasn't outright unfriendly, but we fully understood that providing shelter for us was inconvenient and that they hoped we would soon leave.

They had been able to save their house, all their possessions throughout the war and now were unwilling to part with any part of them, even for other Germans like us who had lost everything and were barely alive. It was as if we all had been shipwrecked and they were the lucky first survivors in the lifeboat, heartlessly clobbering us as we tried to get aboard. There in an area untouched by bombs or invasion, we envied the local inhabitants. I felt as if I were an intruder instead of a human being amongst relatives, family.

Paul obtained ration cards for us, but we couldn't get any basic clothing. Hilda and a neighbor grudgingly gave Paul and me a pair of shoes each. Though worn and ones we never would have kept in former days, we were most grateful. They made us feel as if they had parted with family heirlooms, though I noticed my cousin had many pairs and was far from destitute.

Paul whispered to me the second night, "Hannah, back in 1944 my colleague Mann and I were discussing the end of the war, and he asked me if I would be willing to share my possessions and savings with my countrymen who were being bombed and losing all they had, like my sister Grete, who has even less than we. At that time Silesia was relatively safe, and we did not know the Russians would invade, let alone the Poles."

"What was your answer?"

"I told him I would be willing to sacrifice half of what I had."

"Now we're the ones in need."

"And what a shameful show we are presenting to the rest of the world. Other countries are watching Germany, like watching a snake writhing with a shovel holding it to the ground. It is struggling, whole but ready to be cut in half."

"Do you really think the situation is that bad?"

"There may be hatred coming, those who lost little or nothing against those who lost everything, like us. It will be as it was when the Nazis divided the country. Germany will soon be engaged in an inner struggle, will carry a spiritual burden."

On the fifth day, we felt so unwanted that we had to leave, even though Fritzi had barely recovered. Informed of our plans, Hilda said that we really shouldn't plan to stop at other farmhouses and expect the kind treatment we'd just received. Her neighbors had told her that when they saw *Flüctlinge* approach, they went inside and closed the doors. If anyone knocked, they wouldn't answer.

8 AUGUST TO 31 DECEMBER

We walked again, this time without fear of being molested or of being put into a camp, or of being sent back into the Russian zone or of being robbed. There in the British zone we had a tremendous sense of freedom, even of victory, although we were on the losing side.

The British had set up temporary housing for refugees. We were placed in a stable and didn't know for how long. I truly don't think they counted on hundreds of thousands of émigrés from Poland, from Prussia, and from Czechoslovakia descending upon them. Some brought cholera and typhus.

Only too fresh in my memory were the refugees who fled ahead of the Russians through our town. There we were deprived, had little or nothing to share. Here the self-satisfied locals grumbled and complained, but the English always acted correctly and with good will. Had those Germans been living under Russian occupation and approached the enemy's garrison as we now did, they probably would have been imprisoned, if not shot.

Paul became bitter, demoralized. The British could not adequately deal with the influx. They assigned us to barns, large farm houses, school houses, and whatever other buildings would accommodate the thousands pouring into their zone. We refugees compassionately helped each other in our self-sacrificing way.

I had no opportunity to cook, no pots or pans, very little coal, even though we had a permit to buy it, and just a bit of wood. Had I asked Cousin Hilda for an old pot or pan, she probably would have refused. Paul had to wait two months to obtain a permit to buy coal for our communal shelter. When he finally was granted the permit, no coal was available. Then the permit expired. Our ration cards were useless because we needed coats, hats, blankets, and shoes. None of those items were available. As fall came on, we were hungry and cold.

Our former bank account was *kaputt*, and our money from the Russians had been spent. Fortunately we got a small stipend from time to time because I'd applied to the local authorities to become a substitute teacher. My services were needed, but not I. The rejection by the parents degenerated into exactly the hatred Paul had predicted. We even were told to go back to where we came from, that no one had invited us. Somehow we tolerated hunger and malnutrition, but the psychological suffering we experienced from fellow Germans was almost worse than the physical suffering from Russians and Poles.

I watched the mothers of my pupils. They lived in their untouched houses with all their clothing, with all their sheets, with all their blankets, with all their furniture, with all their dishes and pots. Also still intact were their incomes and their bank accounts; yet we had nothing. They had not suffered cruel invaders; they had not been forced from their homes; they had not been terrorized daily. And these were the people who had promoted Hitler's political machine. They maintained that der Fuhrer had lost the war, not that he had started it. I'm sure they still believed the German race would rise again.

As before, we didn't know our neighbors. Had their children been in youth movements? Were the men former storm troopers, Party members, Gestapo guards? Did they feel any remorse that their misdeeds had caused so much suffering to so many? Or did they simply feel anger at having lost? Would they become unreconstructed Nazis?

All of us in the refugee camps were "displaced people." Some were "emigrees" who voluntarily left their homeland. Some of us were expelled; some of us fled. There were differences. "*Flüctlinge*" to the local Germans didn't mean refugees or those fleeing; it meant rubble left over from the war, "white trash."

Paul mused, "People used to establish roots. They stayed in one place. They were compassionate. They had a homeland. We have to face the truth. We are homeless, just three amongst millions of pauperized wanderers. I see only dark clouds."

I tried to cheer him. "We'll find a new kind of life. We still have our rich memories and each other. Some day again you'll have pleasure in teaching and research. No one can take away my love of literature and art and music. I can still envision paintings. I can still hear melodies. I can still recall plots of novels and poems. We have our joy in raising our son and seeing him develop. Our lives are loaded with valuable baggage."

1965

DECEMBER

I'm in California visiting the woman whose family sent us packages in the late 1940's. It's been exactly 20 years since we left the British encampment and were located in public housing in Bremen. We never did make it to Hamburg, which we learned had been heavily bombed.

On my way here I changed planes in Amsterdam. While sitting in the waiting room, I overheard part of a conversation between a man and woman. His voice was extremely loud.

"My dear *fraulein,* I can help you find your college friend in Germany."

Unable to hear her clearly, I next heard:

"I was a German police detective. I won many honors for my abilities to solve cases that no one else could. I can see that you are a very intelligent woman, and I am a very intelligent man. Perhaps that's why we were attracted to each other on the plane."

Each word was a drum beating steadily at the door where I had locked away the past. I didn't want to open that passageway. I didn't want to see the speaker. I knew who he was. Immediately, pulling my hat low over my face, I moved to the other side of the terminal.

Soon my flight was called, and I quickly boarded. With my face shielded by a book, I didn't watch to see if he was on my plane or not. Then I reprimanded myself for silly vanity. How would he recognize me after all this time?

The war is far behind me now. Looking back, I don't know what I expected, if anything, to turn around my life and fortune.

I've searched for my identity. My name was Hannah Vogelsang. It's an old German name, Johannah, but not an old family name, just one my mother liked. I never gave it much thought, but now in my twilight years, I like its sound. Hah Nah. Like a sigh at the end of a day. Not tired, but just resigned. "Vogelsang" means bird song. All bird songs are not chirpy and happy. Mine is more like that of the mourning dove. In fact, I also look like that bird, rather gray, nearly invisible in the small world that I inhabit, unnoticed in the shrubs.

In Bremen Paul received an appointment in a *gymnasium* [high school] to teach science, and eventually I, too, qualified for teaching. Fritzi spent months at a time in a tuberculosis sanitarium, but he overcame his difficulties and earned a law degree. Several years ago I lost Paul to cancer.

His passing first wasn't a surprise, considering that he was 20 years older. The surprise was coming to terms with my emotions. I loved him with all my heart and soul. And I always had. Although I wasn't on board for all the decisions he made, or how he made them, I know that behind them was his love for me and our son. Right or wrong? Who's to say now?

It's a relief that caring for others has come to an end and that I am in California. After a short walk along the shore, I've found a bench. From here I can look far to the horizon and feel in touch with eternity.

Author's Note

In expanding and translating an original journal, I have taken the liberty to change names of people and some places. Because the original manuscript covered only events that happened in 1945, I have also added historical material and created fictitious background material for my characters. In no way have my additions altered the authenticity of events presented.